tasks for teacher education

a reflective approach

trainer's book

rosie tanner and catherine green

Addison Wesley Longman Limited
Edinburgh Gate, Harlow
Essex CM20 2JE, England
and Associated Companies throughout the world.

© Addison Wesley Longman Limited 1998

The rights of Catherine Green and Rosie Tanner to be identified as authors of this Work have been asserted by them in accordance with the Copyright, Designs and Patents Act 1988

All rights reserved; no part of this publication may be reproduced, stored in a retrieval system, or transmitted in any form or by any means, electronic, mechanical, photocopying, recording or otherwise (except as granted below), without the prior written permission of the Publishers.

Permission to copy
The Publishers grant permission for the photocopying of those pages described as 'Photocopy Masters' according to the following conditions. Individual purchasers may make copies for their own use or for use by classes they teach. School purchasers may make copies for use by their staff and students, but this permission does not extend to additional schools or branches of an institution, which should purchase a separate master copy of the book for their own use. Under no circumstances may any part of this book be photocopied for resale.

For copying in any other circumstances prior permission in writing must be obtained from Addison Wesley Longman Limited.

First published by Addison Wesley Longman Limited 1998

Set in ITC Stone Serif 9.5/11.5pt
Produced through Longman Malaysia, ACM
Designed by Neil Adams
Illustrations by Chris Pavely

ISBN 0 582 31664 2

Acknowledgements
We are grateful to Teachers of English to Speakers of Other Languages (TESOL) and the authors for permission to reproduce extracts from pp60, 88 and 97 (photocopiable) in Dialogue Journal Writing with Non-native Speakers by Joy Kreeft Peyton and Leslee Reed, 1990 Alexandria VA: TESOL. Copyright 1990 by TESOL.

Photo Acknowledgements
We are grateful to the following for permission to use the copyright photograph:
Addison Wesley Longman/Gareth Boden for page 57

INTRODUCTION

To the trainer using *Tasks for Teacher Education*

Tasks for Teacher Education helps language teacher trainees and teachers to develop into aware, self-critical teachers with a sense of self-direction. It contains a wide range of practical tasks which trainees experience as learners and teachers and is designed mainly for pre-service trainees and teachers of English as a foreign language and English as a second language. It may also be adapted for use by trainees and teachers of other foreign languages.

Using *Tasks for Teacher Education*

Each of the sixteen self-contained units deals with one topic and provides a variety of practical tasks which raise awareness and encourage self-direction. *Tasks for Teacher Education* is designed so that the units may be used separately and in any order: you do not need to do every activity in each unit but you can do those tasks which are appropriate to your own context. Each unit begins with a Map, which gives an overview of the whole unit and each separate task. The tasks in *Tasks for Teacher Education* have been used by teacher trainees in many different contexts and countries, from lengthy pre-service courses to weekend in-service sessions. Further information on the tasks can be found on pages v-vi in the trainees' book.

The trainer's notes

The trainer's notes help you to guide trainees through the units. These notes are included in the trainer's book only and contain:

- easy-to-follow directions for facilitating tasks
- aim(s) of each task
- the timing of each task
- suggestions for leading tasks
- ways of concluding tasks
- key issues to draw to trainees' attention
- sample answers where appropriate.

Your role as trainer

Tasks for Teacher Education encourages you as a trainer to be a facilitator rather than an expert, helping your trainees to develop awareness about teaching and themselves as teachers. One definition of a facilitator is 'a person who has the role of helping participants to learn in an experiential group' (Heron 1992:11). The trainer's aim in using this book is, therefore, to allow trainees to experience a task and to draw their own conclusions about their learning. You may, however, wish to voice your own opinion once a task is completed.

Photocopiable material

The photocopiable material section, supplied as photocopy masters for ease of use, can be found at the end of the trainer's book only (pages 49-96); these masters include, for example, observation tasks, role cards, information gap tasks, games, a transcription of a real lesson and pictures. For many of the tasks you need to provide photocopies from this section for your trainees; in some cases, for example for some microteaching tasks or for observation tasks used to observe teaching, trainees need instructions or photocopiable materials in advance.

We hope that you and your trainees will enjoy using the tasks in *Tasks for Teacher Education: A reflective approach*. On page vii in the trainees' book you can find our contact address: we would very much welcome your or your trainees' feedback on any aspect of our book.

Note: there are two kinds of page references in these trainer's notes: the main one refers to pages in the trainees' book (e.g. pages 6-7); the second, marked with the letter T, refers to pages in the trainer's book (e.g. page T40).

Trainer's notes

1 FIRST THINGS FIRST
The first lesson

In this unit... trainees work on what to do in first lessons.

Reflection

TASK 1 The first time ever I saw your face
(page 1)   20-30 min

The aims of this activity are for trainees to reflect on their own experiences of first lessons and for them to get to know each other.

Step 1   **I**

As an introduction, you could tell trainees about a first lesson outside the context of English teaching that you have experienced.

Step 2   **G** and **I**

Hold a plenary to share ideas.

Beliefs about first lessons

TASK 2 Digging deeper *(page 2)*   20-30 min

This task aims to get trainees thinking about the beliefs behind teachers' actions in first lessons.

Step 1   **P**

1 Some possible answers; accept other reasonable ones:

1 a i h	4 b g	7 h
2 a i	5 k	8 a b c g k
3 d e h	6 c e f g h j	

Step 2   **G**

Hold a plenary to ask for some responses to question 2.

Tasks for first lessons

TASK 3 Starting out *(pages 3-5)*   60 min

This task aims to evaluate different activities for first lessons.

Step 1   **G**

Hold a plenary to discuss answers to the Focus questions. Some possible answers:

1 *Activity*   *Aim(s)*

A	to relax Ls; to get Ls talking immediately; to practise question forms
B	to establish a code of conduct; to give Ls responsibility for their own code of conduct
C	to relax Ls; to get to know each other's names
D	to get Ls talking immediately; to practise question forms
E	to practise YES/NO questions; to learn about Ls' English learning experiences; group co-operation; to write a short paragraph
F	to practise question forms; to get to know something about Ls' personal lives

2 *Activity*   *Age, level, type of learner*

A	16+, intermediate or above, Ls who are strangers to each other
B	children; low intermediate or above
C	children; possibly some adults; beginners; Ls who are strangers to each other
D	12+; low intermediate or above; Ls who are strangers to each other
E	12+; low intermediate or above; Ls who are probably strangers to each other
F	16+; intermediate or above; Ls who are probably strangers to each other

Answers to questions 3 and 4 will vary. For 5 and 6 accept any preferences: different activities will suit teachers working in different situations.

Step 2   **P**

Below are some suggested answers; others are possible.
(i) B; C   (ii) C   (iii) E; F   (iv) B; E   (v) F
(vi) F   (vii) A; D

Microteaching

TASK 4 First impressions *(page 6)*   60 min or more

The aim of this task is for trainees to design and teach an activity for a first lesson. It helps if trainees are familiar with the activities in **Task 3 Starting out** (pp. 3-5). If you are new to microteaching, read **3. Microteaching tasks** and **4. Feedback questions** on pages v-vi of the introduction in the Coursebook.

Step 1   **P**

You might like to give trainees this for homework.

Step 2   **M**

Feedback at this stage should be very supportive and concentrate on the effectiveness of the activity taught rather than the teacher, especially if the class is experiencing microteaching and feedback for the first time.

Time out, take five

Journal entry: My first class as a teacher trainee
(page 6)   10 min

If this is your first experience as a trainer with journal writing, read the section **2. Time out, take five: Journal writing** in the Introduction (p. v) and **Task 7 Very truly yours** (pp. 89-90) in **Unit 11 Right on!** Decide in advance whether you wish individual writers to circulate their entries among the class and, if so, how. Allow them time, either at home or at the end of the session, to reflect in writing on the topics.

2 MIRROR, MIRROR, ON THE WALL...
Classroom observation

In this unit... trainees are introduced to one of the important ideas in this book, namely that observing other teachers and being observed can be a tremendous learning experience for both sides.

Reflection

TASK 1 Picture this *(page 7)*
10-20 min   **I** and **P**

This fantasy activity aims to draw out from trainees their initial, personal reactions to the idea of being observed.

Hold a plenary after trainees have completed the task. Discussion of trainees' answers can lead to the notion that many teachers tend to see observation as something that is judgmental, subjective, and intimidating. However, in this book, these characteristics are more often associated with evaluation than with observation (see the reading in **Task 3 Apples and oranges?** (p. 11) for more on observation versus evaluation).

TASK 2 True confessions *(pages 7-8)*
15 min   **I** and **G**

The aim of this reading activity is to raise trainees' awareness further about their own feelings about being observed.

Observation vs. evaluation

TASK 3 Apples and oranges? *(pages 8-9)*   30-45 min

The purpose of this task is to help trainees distinguish between observation and evaluation.

Step 1   **G**

Go over the examples in the table (p. 9) before trainees work in groups. Monitor the groups carefully and help them to come up with ideas – it might be difficult for them. Some possible responses are in the table on page T6.

Step 2   **I**

Allow ten minutes for individual reading of text on page 11 and class discussion of any additional information or related questions.

Alternative: Assign this reading as homework.

6 TRAINER'S NOTES

Observation	Evaluation

1 • describes an action or behaviour
  • provides concrete information about what occurs in the classroom (% of teacher talking time, etc.)
  • is not intended for use in evaluating a teacher's performance
  • may serve as a mirror for the person teaching or for the person observing
  • can be used for research and learning
2 • focuses on one or many different acts or ways of behaviour
  • may not necessarily be focused on the teacher, but could be on the learners, their interaction, use of equipment, etc.
3 may be done by a teacher trainee, a fellow teacher, a parent or a school inspector
4 can take many different forms, from simple to complex
5 can be done at any time a teacher wants information about her class
6 teacher may see the observation form before or afterwards
7 discussion may occur immediately after the observation or a bit later
	1 • judges an action or behaviour
	  • is primarily used to judge the quality of teacher or learner performance in the classroom
	  • can serve as a record of the teacher's work which then could be used for promotion, firing, etc.
	
	2 may be broad or narrow in focus, though general is more common
	
	3 is usually done by a teacher's superior
	4 can take many different forms, such as charts with grades (numbers, adjectives, etc.) and/or written comments
	5 is usually done whenever a supervisor wants to (e.g. at the end of a year's performance)
	6 teacher often sees the evaluation form afterwards
	7 a discussion often occurs shortly after the lesson or is scheduled for a later appointment

Evaluating

TASK 4 Shifting viewpoints *(pages 9-10)* 45-60 min

This task aims to provide trainees with a taste of being on both the evaluator's and the teacher's side of the fence in a post-lesson discussion. In a role-play, trainees evaluate a part of a lesson from the point of view of one of the following four individuals:

1 an enthusiastic teacher who feels her lesson has been a real success
2 a self-critical teacher who feels her lesson has not gone very well
3 a supportive evaluator who provides positive feedback
4 a negative evaluator who provides negative, critical feedback.

To simulate the lesson that the 'evaluator' has just seen the 'teacher' give, you can use:

a a tape-recording of ten minutes of a lesson, *or*
b a transcript of the lesson on page T50, *or*
c ten minutes of a lesson on video.

Step 1

1 Divide the class into four groups and give each group their role card (p. T49) or hand out copies. At this stage, all the members of each group have the *same* role card (i.e. everyone in Group 1 has the role card **Group 1: Role 1** Enthusiastic teacher). As much as possible, make sure there are equal numbers of teachers and evaluators.

2 Ask trainees to 'observe' the lesson, i.e. to watch or listen to part of a lesson, or to read the transcript of the lesson. They should keep their role in mind and take notes while observing.

3 Give trainees about ten minutes to discuss and take notes on their role and their reactions to the lesson in the light of their role card.

Step 2

1 Pair one teacher with one evaluator so that everyone has a partner. You can choose how to divide the pairs up – critical teacher with supportive evaluator, critical teacher with critical evaluator, etc. Form groups of three with any remaining trainees.

2 Start the role-play and allow it to continue for about five or more minutes, as needed.

Optional follow-on (5 min): Staying in the same role, different pairs repeat the role-play. The aim of this

2 MIRROR, MIRROR, ON THE WALL...

follow-on is to allow trainees to experience different types of reactions to the observed lesson.

Step 3   **G**

Divide the class as far as possible into groups of four, each new group containing one person from each original group. Trainees explain what their roles were and discuss the statements and questions.

Step 4   **C**

Hold a plenary about the differences between observation and evaluation by discussing the Focus questions. Possible points:

1 Evaluations may be a mixture of positive and negative. They do not only have to point out a teacher's shortcomings.

2 An evaluator's words may have a strong emotional impact on the instructor, and hearing them can be very stressful.

3 Various cultural rules of behaviour may exist and be influential (e.g. a teacher is considered a subordinate who should respect and accept the opinion of her evaluator/supervisor even if it conflicts with her own view of her work).

4 A lesson may be judged only partially because of an evaluator's particular interest or viewpoint.

5 There are different times when a discussion on the lesson could be scheduled. Discussing a lesson soon after it occurs may help both parties discuss it more accurately since they can recall the lesson more readily than they could a week later. Discussing it later gives time for reflection.

Observing

TASK 5 Excuse me, may I come in?
(page 10)   15-20 min

This task aims at eliciting the trainees' ideas about how they should approach a teacher whose lesson they wish to observe.

Step 1   **G**

Clarify the task by first going over the examples with trainees.

Step 2   **C**

Hold a plenary to collate ideas.

Some possible responses are listed in the table below.

Note: In any follow-up discussion that occurs with the teacher, trainees should be aware of the language they use when they discuss the lesson with the teacher, being tactful and objective and focusing on observable acts. This can be quite tricky. For example, the trainee could say, *I noticed that the learners participated a lot in your class* (neutral observation) instead of *Your learners were really noisy.* (negative value judgement). Or the trainee might say *They mostly spoke in their native language, didn't they?* (neutral observation) rather than *Why don't you get them to speak English all the time?* (accusation).

Task 5 Excuse me, may I come in?

What?	Why?
1 who you are (name, school, position)	1 identify yourself to teacher
2 why you want to observe her class	2 training purposes: e.g. class assignment, personal growth, see a more experienced teacher
3 when you would like to observe (date, time)	3 clarify your respective needs: uncover any schedule conflicts
4 what in particular you want to observe (level, age, any focus)	4 put teacher's mind at ease; may give trainee valuable information related to it
5 how long you want to observe (e.g. first 15 min., whole class)	5 eliminate any surprises and consequent worries or misgivings on teacher's part
6 whether you want to meet her afterwards (if so, where and when)	6 clarify purpose of post-lesson discussion (also accommodate scheduling of it)
7 where you should sit in her class (keep in mind any need to observe Ls' faces or hear their voices, etc.)	7 put teacher's mind at ease; enable her to help you (e.g. extra chair to be obtained)
8 clarify your role during lesson (active participant, passive observer)	8 teacher can incorporate you into lesson or ignore you; needs to clarify same to Ls
9 show teacher the observation form you will use	9 put teacher's mind at ease when she sees you writing in class

8 TRAINER'S NOTES

TASK 6 Telescopic or microscopic viewing?
(pages 10-11)   45 min (excluding observation)

The aim of this task is for trainees to understand the advantages and disadvantages of two types of descriptive observation, one broad and one narrow, after completing one type and discussing the experience with others.

Step 1   **P**

Divide the class into two groups, assign one group **Class observation table A** (p. T51) and the other **Class observation table B: Use of transitions** (p. T52). Pairs of trainees then use their observation tables to observe the same lesson, as follows:

a outside class, trainees observe an actual class, *or*
b inside class, trainees use the transcript of a lesson on page T50, *or*
c trainees view part of a videotaped lesson.

Step 2   **G**

You may wish to hold a plenary to highlight the main points. Possible answers to the Focus questions:

Class observation table A:

a Purpose – to give observer an overall description. PRO or CON

b Ease of use – easy to record brief answers afterwards, others (like question 2) require more time and can't be done during the lesson. CON, until observer practised at it, then possibly PRO
c Relative accuracy – poor to average? Difficult to watch all things at all times and record them simultaneously. Likely that some perceptions/records will be inaccurate. CON
d Answers will vary.

Class observation table B: Use of transitions:

a Purpose – to give the observer a specific, measured description of one aspect of the lesson. PRO or CON
b Ease of use – Relatively easy, although observer must read instructions first. PRO
c Relative accuracy – Fairly good. Observer focused on one area, not as distracted as in A. PRO
d Answers will vary.

Time out, take five

Journal entry: Nerves of steel *(page 11)*   10 min

Trainees reflect on how their feelings and thoughts about observation have changed since they began this unit, as well as how confident they now feel about observations.

3 GRASPING GRAMMAR
Presenting structures

In this unit... trainees learn about different ways of presenting grammar and practise presentations themselves. The unit assumes that, at some stage, teachers will be presenting grammar to their learners within the approach they are using. It does not deal with grammar practice.

Reflection

TASK 1 What's grammar got to do with it?
(page 13)   20 min

This reflection task asks trainees to think about the role of grammar. Although in the 1970s there was a swing away from explicit grammar teaching, it is now believed that it can be useful to teach grammar within a communicative framework.

Step 1   **I**

Give trainees time to read the quotes and to write down their own view about the role of grammar.

Step 2   **C**

In class discuss what trainees have written; ask trainees to justify what they have written, with examples.

Microteaching

TASK 2 Making connections
(page 14)   60–90 min (excluding microteaching)

The aim of this task is for trainees to reflect on what effective presentation techniques are and to present a new grammar point themselves.

Step 1

Hold a plenary before going on to the microteaching.

Some possible answers:
- use visual aids
- give lots of examples
- let Ls practise or communicate with the new language
- explain in L1
- contrast new grammar point with something in L1
- show how the grammar point is used (e.g. by using a text)
- limit yourself to one or two aspects of the new grammar point
- elicit from learners what they already know
- give encouraging feedback if Ls don't understand the first time
- use humour/fun

Step 2

Trainees can prepare at home or in class. Remind them of the discussion in Step 1 and of the time limit (ten minutes).

Step 3

Groups work simultaneously, each trainee teaching their ten-minute lesson to their peers in turn and then receiving feedback using the Feedback questions (p. 14). To keep the pace going, timekeepers time each teacher strictly during the microteaching.

Presenting

TASK 3 Let me count the ways...
(pages 14–19) 60 min

The aim of this task is for trainees to evaluate twelve different ways of presenting one grammar point (the present perfect), shown on pages 16-19, and for them to decide which ones they would use as a teacher.

Step 1

Possible answers are shown in the table on page T10.

Step 2

In a plenary, ask some trainees to explain their choice of presentation techniques.

TASK 4 Getting it across *(page 20)* 20 min

The aim of this task is to show trainees the importance of presenting both the form and the use of a new grammar item.

Key:

1 *Using a song text* unclear; it depends on the chosen text
2 *Using a time line* unspecified time in the past
3 *Reading* something started in the past which is still true now
4 *Using a picture* unspecified time in the past
5 *Using realia* unspecified time in the past
6 *Personalising* used with *just* to talk about something that has happened in the very recent past
7 *Explaining directly* unspecified time in the past and something started in the past which is still true now
8 *Practising and presenting* questions and tag questions; general questions in the past with *ever*
9 *Discovering* unspecified time in the past and something started in the past which is still true now
10 *Using a chart* unspecified time in the past and general questions
11 *Eliciting* unspecified time in the past
12 *Comparing L1 and L2* unclear (presumably all uses)

TASK 5 Jumbled grammar *(page 21)* 20 min

The aim of this task is to re-order a jumbled grammar presentation and to evaluate it.

Step 1

You will need to copy and cut up enough copies of the jumbled lesson plan on page T53, one plan per pair.

Key: One possible order for the lesson is:
m n a d i e h c g b k l j f

Step 2

Key:

1 *a* Techniques used: Using pictures (the photo in stage a); eliciting (stages d, j, l); explaining directly (stage e); personalising (stages j and f).
b Reasons: Pictures engage Ls' interest and focus them at the beginning of the lesson; both visual and auditory learners will gain from different types of presentations. T has staged the lesson so Ls are gradually producing the target language in a freer way as the lesson progresses.

2 Other presentation techniques used: Listening to texts (stages b, h, k); role-play (stage f); matching (stage g); filling in gaps (stage k).

3 Possible addition: Bring into class more pictures of conversations and guess the dialogues people are having with each other with *Would you like to...?* Some Ls demonstrate their dialogues to the class.

This new stage could be situated between stages d and i.

10 TRAINER'S NOTES

Key to Task 3, Let me count the ways, Step 1

Technique	Advantages	Possible problems
1 Using a song text	• song text is motivating for Ls • Ls can see grammar in context in the song	• focus of lesson might be unclear • subject-matter or slang might be (culturally) inappropriate
2 Using a time line	• clear visual demonstration of tense	• questionable whether Ls will understand by the end of the lesson • no context provided • concept of a time line (and not a circle or a spiral) is culturally dependent
3 Reading	• Ls work things out for themselves • realistic text used • text good for school pupils	• rather contrived text • use of item is not always clear in a text
4 Using a picture	• visual might help visual learners remember • Ls involved in eliciting process • Ls use the tense	• might be hard for some Ls to make sentences • visuals do not necessarily give a clear context
5 Using realia	• shows meaning clearly • involves Ls • Ls might remember better • Ls' examples are used as models	• inadequate demonstration of use • visuals do not necessarily give a clear context
6 Personalising	• learning is related to teacher's and learners' own lives • use is clearly demonstrated • Ls immediately use the tense themselves	• some Ls may not want to answer personal questions or discuss their personal lives
7 Explaining directly	• form on board is clear	• individual Ls might not understand • not many examples given • Ls are not involved
8 Practising and presenting	• uses Ls' real lives • clear explanation given • Ls begin with the use and then learn the form	• Ls might not understand the questions • needs good elicitation techniques from T • Ls have to be used to working in pairs
9 Discovering	• Ls discover meaning for themselves • Ls are familiar with material • recycles material • Ls do a puzzle, so it's perhaps more fun than direct explanation	• text is quite difficult • needs good instruction-giving • could be problematic if learners guess wrongly
10 Using a chart	• Ls involved from the start • clear visual to demonstrate text • Ls practise themselves	• questions and affirmative sentences being presented at same time might confuse some Ls
11 Eliciting	• Ls involved from the start • T discovers what Ls already know	• some Ls might not follow very well
12 Comparing L1 and L2	• useful technique for monolingual class	• not possible with multilingual class • there might be no equivalent in L1

Eliciting and observation

The tasks in this section deal with eliciting, which is an important skill for a teacher to be able to adopt at any time when teaching, but particularly useful if introducing something new.

TASK 6 Drawing it out *(page 21)* 40-80 min

This task focuses on eliciting. Elicit from the trainees reasons for eliciting (e.g. to lead into an activity.).

Step 1

Go over the procedure and purpose of the task before trainees observe. Trainees will each need a copy of the **Observation table: eliciting** (p. T54).

Step 2

Collect trainees' responses or ask them to discuss their answers in class.

Step 3   **G**

Some effective eliciting techniques:

- Remain silent when it is obvious a learner is still thinking.
- If a learner cannot answer, ask another learner.
- Effective questions: *Does anyone know...?; Can anyone tell me...?; Do you know...?; Tell me...*
- Use encouraging language, e.g. *Well done! Great work!*
- If a learner is halfway to an answer, encourage her further by giving some prompts.
- If a learner is almost right, tell her *Not quite*, smile and encourage her further.
- Use intonation to indicate which part of a sentence is correct or incorrect.
- Write a half-right answer on the board and encourage learners to correct it.
- Don't immediately give the answer.
- If a learner is wrong, gently ask another learner to answer.
- If a learner is wrong, ask her to try to correct herself.
- Reject learners' wrong responses in a tactful way.

TASK 7 The eliciting game   **G**
(page 22)   40-60 min

The aim of this game is for trainees to practise eliciting grammar points. Make sure that trainees understand the rules of the game before they begin. As they play, monitor and be ready to suggest improvements as you listen. Have a round-up plenary to make any generally applicable comments.

You will need to prepare the cards for **The Eliciting Game**: copy and cut up one set of Eliciting cards (p. T55) per group of trainees. (You might like to mount them onto cardboard for future use.) The examples on the cards are for teachers teaching at beginner and near-beginner level; if your trainees are likely to teach at higher levels, make a similar set of cards using more complex grammar points; you could also ask trainees to create, say, five cards each for grammar points which they might use.

As a conclusion to the unit, trainees can design a grammar presentation lesson.

4 HOW DO YOU DO?
Introducing vocabulary

In this unit... trainees learn about presenting new vocabulary.

Reflection

TASK 1 At first sight   **I** and **G**
(pages 23-24)   10-15 min

The aim of this task is for trainees to relate how they learn vocabulary to effective ways of presenting vocabulary.

If you have done **Unit 3 Grasping grammar** (pp. 13-22), remind trainees of relevant presentation techniques learnt there.

After trainees have done Steps 1 and 2, hold a plenary so that the whole class can collect together a list of effective presentation techniques for vocabulary, e.g.:

Effective presentation techniques should
- not be too long
- include enough and relevant examples
- include clear/interesting visuals
- use drama
- include clear explanations
- contrast with L1
- link to previously-learnt material
- include interaction (with each other and with words)
- be involving
- include practice
- be an effective check of understanding
- be meaningful
- be amusing, interesting
- hold attention
- be memorable, dramatic, exciting
- use or link to Ls' present knowledge.

Presenting vocabulary

TASK 2 Mark my words *(pages 24-28)*   30-40 min

This task introduces trainees to several ways of presenting the meaning of new vocabulary.

Step 1   **P**

Hold a brief plenary to ask trainees for responses to the Focus questions and their opinions about the techniques; answers will be individual.

Step 2   **P** and **C**

1 Some possible responses:

(a) 5, 1; (b) 2, 5; (c) 1, 3; (d) 1, 6, 9; (e) 6 (f) 1, 8;
(g) 1, 7, 9; (h) 8; (i) 1, 8; (j) 4, 6; (k) 5, 6; (l) 5, 6

2 It is important for trainees to role-play and not only tell about their presentations; that way, you can see how clearly they can present vocabulary.

TASK 3 Double check *(page 28)*   **G**   10-15 min

The aim of this task is to practise concept checking. First ensure that trainees understand the term concept checking, by looking in the Glossary or by explaining it yourself; elicit some practical examples.

Lexical sets

The following two tasks deal with lexical sets: what they are, why they are important and how to teach them.

TASK 4 Why lexical sets? *(page 29)*   **I**   10 min

First ask trainees to think about question 1 and then hold a brief plenary before trainees read.

This reading is linked to the Microteaching in **Task 5 Choice of words**, which involves teaching a lexical set; it demonstrates the importance of presenting words in groups, rather than as isolated items.

Microteaching

TASK 5 Choice of words *(page 30)*   40-50 min

This task highlights some of the difficulties in presenting new vocabulary to learners and gets trainees thinking about further effective presentation techniques.

Step 1   **C**

With the class, quickly choose a lexical set to base the microteaching on (e.g. *a lexical set of furniture: table, chair, sofa, armchair, carpet, television, curtains, coffee table, rug, telephone*).

Step 2   **G** and **M**

1 Remind trainees of the other tasks in this unit (2 and 3) which deal with vocabulary presentation.

2 Ensure that the lesson plans are clear and understandable. As you monitor, decide on which plan to use for the microteaching and select one trainee to teach.

3 The trainee teaches the vocabulary lesson strictly according to the lesson plan.

Step 3   **C**

Groups discuss the Feedback questions in class after the microteaching. In a plenary discussion, you can use the questions to:

- collect together some useful presentation techniques
- discuss what effective learning occurred and why
- discuss how the lesson plan might be improved.

5 WARMING UP
Teaching the four skills: task preparation

In this unit... trainees experience, read about, discuss, design, evaluate and teach warming-up activities.

Reading

TASK 1 Why warm up? *(pages 31-32)*   15 min

This reading passage links real life and language learning, and explains the importance of preparing learners to do language work.

Step 1   **P**

Discuss trainees' answers before they read.

Step 2   **I**

After reading, discuss trainees' answers in class.

Observation

TASK 2 Do as I say (*pages 32-33*)   30 min or more (excluding observation)

This observation task looks at several aspects of instruction giving and aims to discover what the trainees themselves value in instruction giving. It is a relatively judgmental task, unlike other observation tasks in this book, which aim to be more objective. It is not necessarily true that a teacher using all of the skills will be good at giving instructions.

Step 1   **G** and **C**

The aim of this step is to warm up before the observation task.

Step 2   **I**

Trainees will each need several copies of the **Observation table: Instruction-giving skills** (p. T56) to observe different activities in the lesson. They can also use one copy of the table, with different colours representing different activities. Review the task together in class before they observe.

Alternative tasks:
a Trainees observe, using the transcript on page T50.
b A few trainees do this observation task during the microteaching task in **Task 5 Paving the way**, Step 3.

Step 3   **I**

Trainees can either discuss their answers to the Post-observation questions in a plenary or give you a copy of their written answers.

Step 4   **C**

A further discussion could concern what *other* elements *not* mentioned in the observation task can also be important for effective instruction giving (for example, readiness of learners to listen or to cooperate; the effectiveness of using L1 or L2 for instructions).

Pre-reading

TASK 3 Before you read (*pages 33-35*)   60 min

The aim of this task is for trainees to experience a pre-reading activity and to reflect on that experience.

Step 1   **G**

Accept any ideas here; the aims of this activity are (a) to give the trainees a reason for reading (they will want to find out if their guesses are correct) and (b) to interest them in the topic of pre-reading.

Step 2   **I**

Trainees can read the article (p. 34) in class or at home. Check their predictions from Step 1.

Step 3   **C** and **I** or **P**

Key:

1 The pre-reading activity introduces trainees to some of the vocabulary and the topics in the text and perhaps motivates them to want to read further.

2 Answers will be individual.

3 Trainees can prepare the pre-reading activity in class or at home, individually or in pairs.

4 Organise an exchange of ideas after trainees have designed their activities.

Pre-listening

TASK 4 Forearmed (*pages 35-37*)   40-50 min

In this task, trainees analyse five different pre-listening activities.

Step 1   **P**

Discuss your trainees' answers and perhaps complete the table together in plenary. Some suggested answers to question 3 are shown in the table on page T14.

Step 2   **G**

This step aims to link the two parts of the unit dealing with warming up for receptive skills activities.

Some similarities between warming-up activities for reading and listening:

- both deal with a text
- activities can use any of the four skills
- warming-up activities often involve guessing or predicting about the topic or language in a text
- activities can use words from the texts to be read or listened to.

14 ◆ TRAINER'S NOTES

Key to Task 4, Forearmed, Step 1

Pre-listening activity	Aim(s) of activity	Skill(s) practised
A Using pictures	1 to contextualise the listening text 2 to motivate learners to want to listen	writing, speaking
B Personalising	1 personalising the topic by bringing in a real-life story 2 motivating learners	speaking, listening
C Predicting vocabulary	1 to interest/motivate learners 2 to give learners a reason for listening	speaking
D Predicting facts	1 to intrigue/interest learners 2 to contextualise the listening text	speaking, writing
E Practising tenses	1 to practise simple past tense and negatives in past tense 2 to give learners a reason for listening (to check their answers) 3 to discover the way a text is linked together	reading, writing

Pre-writing and microteaching

TASK 5 **Paving the way**   90-120 min
(pages 38-39)   (excluding preparation)

This task aims to deal with problems that trainees have had in the past with learning to write in another language and suggests that pre-writing activities can often forestall some of these problems. In Step 2, trainees design their own pre-writing activities and in Step 3 they try out their activities by microteaching them.

Step 1   **G**

Hold a plenary to clarify answers.

1 Some more writing problems (you and your trainees will think of others):

- I didn't know what to write – I got 'writer's block'.
- I couldn't organise my work.

2 The general aim for pre-writing can be summed-up in this way: 'the goals are to stimulate and motivate learners to generate materials to write on' (Oluwadiya 1992: 13). In the same article, Oluwadiya states that learners actually write better if they do pre-writing activities. A suggested key:

Problem	Possible pre-writing activity
• I didn't know what to write – I got 'writer's block'.	• Do some free writing: learners write continuously, without thinking, for five minutes.
• I couldn't organise my work.	• Do some planning with the learners; read a model text.

Step 2   **G**

To make sure trainees understand the writing task, ask some short questions, such as:

'What do the learners have to write?' (a dialogue)
'Who is the dialogue between?' (Jerry and his parents)
'What is the problem?' (Jerry arrives home very late and his parents are worried/angry)

The class works in four groups (A, B, C and D) (or eight groups if you have a large class) on pre-writing activities (p. T57). You will need to provide copies. Each group uses and designs a different pre-writing activity, as follows:

Group A: Using a picture
Group B: Listening
Group C: Brainstorming
Group D: Clustering

Give groups a time limit of about 20 minutes for Step 2. The Focus questions on page 38 are there to

5 WARMING UP

help trainees plan their activities. Trainees might need extra support from you with question 6 to clarify the precise aims of their activity.

Step 3   M and C

This step involves trainees microteaching the pre-writing activities prepared in the first half of this task. One group representative microteaches their pre-writing activity to the rest of the class while other group members observe; for example, Group A chooses one of their group to teach the pre-writing activity *Using a picture* while the rest of Group A observes.

Feedback questions

After the microteaching, trainees can work in new groups to discuss the Feedback questions on page 39; encourage positive comments and practical improvements.

Step 2   I and P

Hold a plenary to discuss trainees' answers.

Step 3   G

Some similarities between warming-up activities for speaking and writing:

- often involve practice of speaking or writing
- often involve input (e.g. functions, vocabulary, phrases) to help learners know what to say or write
- can use any of the language skills
- might include mini-exercises which are then put together in the activity.

Additional task

Trainees could design a warming-up activity for homework, based on a coursebook used in your teaching context.

Pre-speaking

TASK 6 Before you open your mouth...
(pages 39-41)   30-40 min

The aim of this task is to evaluate some pre-speaking activities for a role-play.

Step 1   P

In this step, trainees complete the columns **Skill(s) practised**, **Grouping** and **Aim(s)** in the table on page 40; they should ignore the **Rank** column. If you like, hold a plenary to discuss trainees' preferences. In the table below are some possible answers.

Pre-speaking activity	Skill(s) practised	Grouping	Aim(s)
A Eliciting ideas	speaking listening	whole class	• introducing learners to the topic • interesting learners in the topic • predicting contents of a dialogue
B Listening to a dialogue	listening speaking	whole class and pairs	• introduction to the topic • listening for specific information • interesting learners in the topic
C Using key words	writing speaking	pairs	• writing a conversation • introducing the topic • cooperating • problem-solving
D Using photographs	listening	whole class	• revising greetings and telephone language • focusing on the topic

6 NOW HEAR THIS!
Teaching listening

In this unit... trainees learn about teaching listening. See the Glossary (pp. viii-x) for definitions of pre-listening, while listening and post-listening.

Reflection

TASK 1 All ears *(pages 42-43)*   20-30 min

The aim of this task is to compare listening in L1 outside the classroom and listening to English inside the class.

Step 1   G

See possible version of a completed Listening Mind Map below. Accept any reasonable answers.

Step 2   G

Focus questions (possible answers):

1 *Listening to L1 outside the classroom*

- usually not tape-recorded: language is fleeting
- purpose for listening is clear
- listening happens in context
- we listen because we want to
- language is not simplified.

Listening to English inside the classroom

- often relies on a tape, which you can replay
- purpose is not always clear
- listening does not always occur in context
- we listen because the teacher tells us to
- some listening texts are simplified.

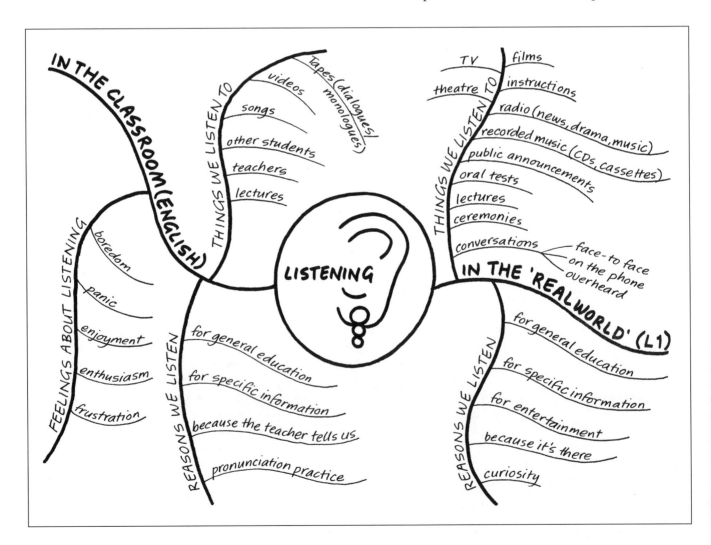

6 NOW HEAR THIS!

2 Give learners their task before they listen, so that they know what they are listening for.

3 • Tell Ls the topic of the listening text and ask them to predict what the text is about.
   • Use a picture to introduce the topic of the listening text or to predict something in the text.
   • Tell Ls why they are listening.
   • Use some of the vocabulary in the text to introduce it (e.g. give some words and ask Ls to predict what the text is about).

4 • Tell Ls it doesn't matter if they don't understand everything in the text.
   • Do some easy listening activities so Ls can succeed, before going on to more difficult ones.
   • Give Ls an easier activity first to get gist of passage.
   • Train Ls to listen first for the general idea of a text.
   • Ask Ls to bring songs to class and do listening tasks with those.
   • Give Ls a purpose for listening (i.e. give them tasks while they listen).
   • Do pre-listening activities to introduce Ls to the text and to contextualise it.
   • Don't just say 'listen to this' – it might panic Ls; always give Ls a task to do.

Step 3   **C**

Hold a brief plenary to discuss answers to Step 2.

Listening tasks

TASK 2 Using an ear trumpet
(pages 44-46)   30-45 mins

The aim of this task is to expose trainees to a variety of listening task types and to develop awareness about their aims.

Step 1   **P**

Possible answers:
1 A, G; 2 B, C, D, E, H, J; 3 F; 4 F, D; 5 I; 6 F; 7 B, C, E; 8 J; 9 G; 10 D, H

Step 2   **G**

Key:
1 *a* A, B, C, E, F, H, I, J
   b A, B, C, D, E, H, I
   c G
   d Ls can listen and respond easily at the same time; drawing or matching responses allows Ls to concentrate on listening to the language of the text.

e In writing long answers or reading long questions, Ls can miss part of the tape; can also miss looking at other questions.

2 and 3 Answers will vary.

Observation

TASK 3 Eavesdropping on a teacher
(page 47)   40 min (excluding observation time)

The aims of this observation task are for trainees to observe a listening lesson and to reflect on it.

Step 1   **I**

Before they observe, clarify the task and show trainees the example in the **Observation table: Teaching listening** (p. T58). They will each need a copy of the table.

Step 2   **I**

Trainees answer the Post-observation questions in writing.

Key

Questions 1 to 4: answers will vary.

5 *a* Possible advantages:
   • Resembles real life in that a context is provided.
   • The class is oriented to the topic of the tape in advance.
   • It builds on what Ls know.
   • Ls succeed better if they concentrate on one task at a time.
   • Can vary the focus in each stage (e.g. from general listening to listening for more specific information).
   • Ls can practise other skills as well as listening.

   b Possible disadvantages:
   • It's not very realistic to listen several times to something.
   • In real life, there is often no time for careful orientation or logical follow-up (e.g. you may hear an announcement at a train station only once, at fast speed).

Listening

TASK 4 And the winner is...
(page 48)   25-30 min

The aim of this task is to evaluate the effectiveness of different teaching listening techniques (p. T59). Hold a plenary to check trainee's answers. Some sample answers are in the table on page T18 (your scores and ideas might be different).

18 TRAINER'S NOTES

Key to Teaching listening techniques

	Score	Advantage(s)	Disadvantage(s)
a	4	—	• no preparation for listening • no purpose stated
b	1	• Ls oriented; more likely to succeed at task	—
c	1	• Ls' background knowledge is tapped • motivates Ls to listen for 'their' words	—
d	1	• questions stimulate Ls' interest in the listening passage • Ls listen for answers to 'their' questions	—
e	4	• Ls focus on global comprehension before doing more detailed listening	• task is not specific
f	1	• Ls are better prepared to understand details once they have clear understanding of whole • clear task is provided	—
g	3	• use of L1 easier for Ls to express themselves • quick way for T to check comprehension	• Ls don't understand their aim or reason for listening • task not specific • Ls not using English
h	2	• may allow for greater comprehension without pressuring Ls to speak before they're ready • accommodates visual learners more	• some Ls might panic about having to draw
i	3	• translation may reveal Ls' knowledge in a quick way	• not a very natural activity • Ls trying to comprehend conversation bit by bit rather than get main idea
j	2	• helps Ls with spelling • Ls concentrate on sounds	• listening once may not give Ls a chance to comprehend whole • Ls concentrating on sounds, not meaning
k	3	• Ls may be experienced at this traditional exercise and able to succeed, based on practice	• no task provided, so the task is testing memory rather than the understanding of spoken language
l	1	• by listening several times, Ls can comprehend the whole message • new purpose each time allows gradual understanding of complete text	• could get boring if tape is easy
m	3	• Ls gain familiarity with text	• not a natural activity • may bore some Ls who comprehend quickly

Microteaching

TASK 5 Tune in
(page 48)   40 min (excluding preparation time)

The aims of this task are (a) for trainees to design
pre-listening, while-listening and post-listening
activities and (b) to experience these, either as
teachers or learners.

Step 1   **G** and **P**

Select six trainees to do Step 1 in advance. Emphasise
the time limits.

Alternative: three volunteers prepare and teach the
listening lesson.

6 NOW HEAR THIS! / 7 SPEAKING YOUR MIND

Step 2 **M**

After the microteaching is completed, lead a follow-up discussion, keeping the trainees' feedback sessions brief and supportive.

Time out, take five

Journal entry: If I had only known then what I know now *(page 49)* **I** 10 min

This journal entry prompts trainees to reflect on what they have learned about teaching listening and what they would still like to know or have clarified.

7 SPEAKING YOUR MIND
Teaching speaking

In this unit... trainees reflect on, experience, evaluate and teach speaking activities. Other units which relate to teaching speaking include Unit 5 Warming up and Unit 12 We all make mistakes.

Reflection

TASK 1 Talking of speaking
(pages 50-51) 20-30 min

The aim of this task is to experience a speaking activity, in order to think about what makes an effective speaking class.

Step 1 **C**

Explain the task to your class, clarify any problems and then do the task.

Step 2 **G**

There are some sample answers in the table below.

Step 3 **C**

Hold a plenary so trainees can add further items to their own lists.

Key to Step 2 (possible answers)

Our criteria for a good speaking class	Our reasons why
The teacher... • should insist on learners speaking English. • should accept answers tactfully, even if they are wrong.	• The learners get a lot of input. • The learners feel accepted and might contribute again in class.
The learners... • need to be tolerant of each other. • should not laugh at each other. • should make an effort to speak English.	 • They might be shy or embarrassed if they are scared of other learners. • So that they will want to speak again. • They will participate more.
The atmosphere... • should be relaxed. • should encourage everyone to participate.	 • If learners feel relaxed, they will contribute more. • If everyone participates, more English is spoken.
Correction... • It's not necessary to correct every single mistake. • The teacher should not correct the learners rudely. • Learners can correct each other.	 • Ls can sometimes be encouraged to speak fluently. • Learners are also people! • They might feel less threatened if corrected by peers, if the teacher and fellow learners are supportive of this.
Activities... • should have lots of pair and group work. • should include interesting discussion topics. • should be varied.	 • So that everyone gets a chance to speak. • To motivate learners. • To prevent boredom.

20 TRAINER'S NOTES

Speaking activities

TASK 2 Filling the gap (pages 51-52)   10-15 min

The aim of this task is to introduce the concept of information gaps and stress their importance in teaching speaking.

Step 1

Elicit these answers as far as possible:

1 Different learners have different information and have to communicate to complete an activity, e.g. learner A has a picture, learner B has to discover what is in the picture; learner A has a form to complete and learner B has the information to complete it.

2 • Learners have to communicate to 'fill the gap'.
  • Learners don't know the answers, so it makes communication more real.
  • Filling information gaps resembles real life.
  • Information-gap activities motivate learners.
  • Learners can work in pairs or groups and therefore speak more English.

Step 2

Key:

1 *a* Yes.
  b Trainees do not know the answers to the questions they ask.

2 *Activity A: Completing a questionnaire*
  a Yes.
  b No-one knows the answers to the questions – only the teacher. The gap is between what the teacher knows and what the learners know.

  Activity B: Having a discussion
  a Yes.
  b The learners don't know what their classmates think about the answers to the questions.

  Activity C: Reading a dialogue aloud
  a No.
  b Both learners can see the dialogue and know what is coming; there is nothing unexpected.

  Activity D: Creating and reading a weather forecast
  a Yes.
  b The partner doesn't know what you have written in your weather forecast.

TASK 3 Talking the hind leg off a donkey
(page 53)   60 min

The aim of this task is for trainees to evaluate three different speaking activities as possible teaching material. To save time, each group can evaluate a different task and report back to the whole class.

Step 1

You will need to provide copies of the table **Talking the hind leg off a donkey** (p. T60) for each pair of trainees.

Hold a plenary discussion to compare ideas.

Some possible answers are in the table on the opposite page (some are, inevitably, subjective).

Step 2

If trainees have not done any work on lesson plans, you might like to suggest what elements they can use for a plan (e.g. stages, materials, aims, timing); look at **Unit 13 Plan of attack** (pp. 98-105) for more ideas.

TASK 4 Talking shop (page 54)   20-30 min

The aim of this task is to think in detail about how to teach a speaking activity (see also **Unit 5 Warming up** (pp. 31-41) for more input on warming-up activities).

Step 1

Hold a brief plenary to ask trainees their own opinions.

Step 2

Some possible answers to the Focus questions:

1 Grammar: present simple questions and 'tag' answers (*Yes, they do; No, they don't*). Vocabulary: everyday language to do with school and home.

2 Ask the class a general question (e.g. *Are your parents strict? Do you agree with their rules for you?*) and have short dialogues with individuals about the rules that their parents have.

3 Divide them clearly into pairs with gestures; any 'extra' learner can join a pair to make a group of three. Divide them after giving instructions for the activity.

4 Do some example open-pair questioning across the class, asking learners to ask each other the first two questions in the activity and showing on the board how they should answer.

5 Answers will vary.

6 Walk around the class monitoring and listening to see if they are using the correct language; collect some mistakes together on a sheet of paper for later feedback.

7 Make some kind of encouraging remark (if they have done it well); use a summarising remark (e.g. *Your parents don't seem very strict!*). Ask for some example answers, asking learners to tell you about the rules of their partner's parents.

8 Ask them to write a paragraph about their partner's parents' rules and perhaps their opinion on these.

7 SPEAKING YOUR MIND 21

Key to Task 3 Talking the hind leg off a donkey, Step 1

	Activity A Drawing a picture	Activity B Role-play	Activity C Parent power
a What language (e.g. grammar, vocabulary, functions) does the activity aim to produce?	Vocab: *buildings, countryside*; Prepositions; *It is/ there is/are.*	Questions mostly in present tense; everyday (home) vocab.	Present tense questions and tag answers.
b How effectively will the activity generate the language that it aims to produce?	Well: restricted task leads to use of language.	Quite well: Ls might limit themselves to vocab on role cards.	Well: very controlled activity.
c What preparation will the class need to do it?	Practise perhaps with teacher giving an example on board; reminder about prepositions and vocab.	Checking of understanding of role cards.	Reminding of present tense questions and tag answers, 'Yes, they do', 'No, they don't'.
d How much will everyone participate in the activity?	Describer will probably say more.	Equal.	Equal amount – but not much (only tag answers).
e Is there an information gap in the activity?	Yes.	Yes.	Yes.
f How much English will the learners speak?	A fair amount, especially the describer.	Quite a lot.	Equal amount – but not much (*Yes, they do/ No, they don't.*)
g How interesting and enjoyable is the activity for your own learners?	Fun: nice for learners to draw picture.	OK – close to their lives perhaps.	Quite; could be problem if Ls don't have 2 parents.
h Do the learners have short or long speaking turns?	Fairly long.	Quite long.	Quite short.
i What problems can you foresee with this activity?	Ls might show pictures; Ls might be scared of drawing.	Ls only read the cards and don't play their roles.	Some Ls might not have many relations or might not like talking about them.

Microteaching

TASK 5 Chatterbox *(page 55)*   40-50 min

The aim of this microteaching task is to experience an information-gap activity using pictures.

Step 1   **M**

The microteaching trainee needs to prepare her lesson in advance of the lesson; give her the **Teacher's instructions** and the pictures on page T61. The rest of the class read the **Learners' instructions** on page 55.

Steps 2 and 3   **G**

After the group discussion, hold a feedback session, encouraging trainees to give tactful and positive comments to the microteaching trainee.

TASK 6 They've lost their tongues
(pages 55-56)   20 min

The aim of this task is to find some solutions to common problems with teaching speaking.

Step 1   **C**

Elicit answers to the questions and draw up a list of problems in teaching speaking.

Step 2   **P**

Some possible responses:

1 a, b, f, j.
2 b, d, e, i.
3 h, i, k.
4 a, b, d, f, j, k.

5 c, g, k.
6 a, b, d, h, i, j.
7 a, i, j.

Step 3 G

Possible answers:

1 Describe the problem with Emil.
   - Emil only speaks English if teacher nearby (but does speak English if teacher is there).
   - He talks too much in L1.
   - Emil's English level is too low for the class.
   - He is maybe scared of speaking English (loss of face with his peers?).
   - He doesn't know what to say.

2 Why do you think this problem exists?
   - Emil has a lively character and likes talking; perhaps he's the clown of the class.
   - He doesn't listen.
   - He's scared of being laughed at by his classmates.
   - He doesn't know what to say in English.
   - He thinks it's silly to speak English.

3 Think of at least **three** different solutions for the problem.
   - Give him an extra task – e.g. to observe something, to be a group secretary or chairman so he has to ask others for their ideas in English.
   - Encourage other learners to encourage him to talk in English or put him in a group where other learners will encourage him to speak.
   - Praise him each time he does speak English.
   - Ask him to say one thing in English in one lesson, two in the next, etc. and praise him for it.
   - Don't answer him or listen to him unless he speaks English; explain to him that others have to have a turn, too.
   - Talk individually but encouragingly to Emil and ask him to change.
   - Be explicit about why you are teaching speaking and why it is important for everyone to speak (e.g. for practice, for exams, for fun).
   - Use three- or four-way information gap tasks so that everyone has to share their information and therefore speak.

You and your trainees will probably think of other solutions appropriate for your teaching context.

Game

TASK 7 The atmosphere game
(pages 56-57)   40-50 min

The aim of this game is for trainees to experience practical ways of establishing and maintaining a good atmosphere as a teacher in class; it focuses on speaking activities, but the theory behind it is applicable to all classroom situations. The game is partly based on Krashen's idea that learners possess an *affective filter*, which allows language acquisition to take place if it is lowered[1]. To lower the filter, the teacher needs to create an environment where anxiety levels are low and where there are good relationships between teacher and learners: when learners feel relaxed, they will then feel able to express their ideas and opinions.

Step 1

This warming-up activity gets trainees thinking about their past experience with teachers who have been able to create a relaxed atmosphere. Ask them to provide very specific examples of how their teachers have done this. Some examples from our experience:

- A teacher talked to the class during coffee breaks and sometimes had lunch with us.
- A teacher asked us genuinely about our lives outside the classroom.

Step 2 G

You will need to provide the materials for the game (pp. T62-63).

Do an example for the class first so that trainees understand that they have to do a mini role-play each time they land on a square, actually saying the words that they would say as a teacher in the situation, e.g.:

On square 3 horizontal, 4 vertical, it says *Give positive feedback to two learners who have voiced opposite opinions on the topic of animal rights.* Role-play an example, saying, *This is what I would say. 'Helena and Joyce, you gave very interesting arguments. Helena, I can understand that you think everyone should have the right to make-up and fur coats and that you believe animals are here for humans to use; that's an interesting idea. But I can also see Joyce's point of view that animals also have rights, just like humans, and that we shouldn't exploit them. Well done, both of you.'*

- On some squares, the other players must provide a topic or a situation or act out a role-play as if they were learners; do an example of one of these.
- Give some examples of each type of feedback (rule 4) so that trainees know what to say at the feedback stage. For example, *You were a bit rude to the learner; could you be a bit more tactful?* or *Your instructions were too long and complex; could you repeat them in a shorter, clearer way?*
- Stop the game when you feel the groups are ready.

Step 3

Some possible pieces of advice (some might be irrelevant to your own context):

- Keep speaking English yourself.
- In a relaxed way, encourage learners to speak English as much as possible.
- Give your learners explanations about why you do something.
- Show an interest in your learners' lives outside class.

[1] Krashen and Terrell, 1983.

7 SPEAKING YOUR MIND / 8 BETWEEN THE LINES — 23

- Share something about your own life with your learners.
- Do not allow learners to be rude to one another.
- Encourage helping between learners.
- Discuss problems with your learners (e.g. if they make you angry or irritated).
- Encourage learners to correct themselves: don't immediately give them the correct answers.
- Be encouraging and give lots of positive feedback about language and how they did during activities.
- Apologise if you do something wrong.
- Be especially tactful and encouraging with shy learners; don't always force them to contribute.

Time out, take five

Journal entry: Writing about speaking
(page 57)   ▌ *10 min*

Trainees reflect upon some of the problems with teaching speaking in the unit and think about whether they believe they have found some solutions.

8 BETWEEN THE LINES
Teaching reading

In this unit... trainees learn about different ways of teaching reading. In Unit 5 Warming Up (pages 31-41), there is more on pre-reading activities. You can find definitions of pre-reading, while-reading and post-reading in the Glossary (pages viii-x).

Observation

TASK 1 Private eye
(pages 58-59)   (30 min excluding observation time)

The aim of this observation task is to compare reading L1 in real life with reading English in the classroom. There are two parts to the observation, one in Step 1 and one in Step 2. You need to give the trainees the two **Observation tables** (pp. T64-65) in advance.

Step 1   ▌

Clarify the observation task, which is done outside the classroom. Trainees will each need a copy of the **Observation table: Real-life reading** (p. T64).

Step 2   ▌

Clarify the observation task, which is done inside the classroom. Trainees will each need a copy of the **Observation table: Classroom reading** (p. T65)

Step 3   ▌

You can collect in trainees' written responses to the Post-observation questions or discuss them in class.

Key:

1 Answers are individual.

2 Reading aloud in the classroom is useful for practising pronunciation. In real life, it is rare that we read aloud; if we do it, we usually read aloud to give someone else information (e.g. a child's bedtime story, an article in the newspaper of interest to someone we are with, a timetable to tell someone the train times).

3 Answers will vary.

4 • Use authentic texts.
  - Vary the purposes of reading and make the purposes clear to learners (e.g. scan a directory for an address you need, skim the back cover of a novel to grasp its plot).
  - Find out why learners want to read and relate purpose of task to their aims.
  - Give Ls more choice in what they read.
  - Create a more relaxed, home-like environment (e.g. add music, more comfortable seating, different postures).

5 • State the aim explicitly (*The purpose of this task is...* or *Your aim in reading this is...*).
  - Give out the text and explain the aim of the task at the same time, rather than after the learners have read the passage.

6 • Create a reading shelf or library in the classroom, consisting of materials learners have contributed.
  - Give Ls time in class to read for pleasure.
  - Ls understand that the skills they develop in reading extensively can benefit them in reading at school (e.g. for English exams).
  - Help Ls make up some questions themselves (ones they genuinely want answers to) before they read, and then read to find those answers.
  - Make a list of English magazines that are available and ask learners to pick one they would like to read, then they report on an aspect of it to the class.
  - Tell Ls titles and some interesting details about some books in English that might interest them.
  - Read aloud short exciting sections of books.

24 ◆ TRAINER'S NOTES

Reflection

TASK 2 The tortoise or the hare?
(page 59)   30-40 min

The aims of this task are (a) to characterise different reading strategies as effective or ineffective (p. T66) and (b) to then identify which of these trainees themselves use when reading. It may be helpful to do this task yourself first in order to provide a model.

Step 1   **P**

Key

See below.

Step 2   **G**

If you wish, hold a brief plenary to discuss your trainees' answers.

Reading Strategies	Effective (E) or Ineffective (I)	Reasons
a	I	Slows reader; eyes move faster than finger; brain can process faster.
b	I	Slows reader. A better way of reading is to get the gist first, to understand context, then make logical guesses from context.
c	E	Understanding main ideas first can help reader understand details later.
d	I	You read more quickly with your eyes alone than if you mouth the words.
e	I	Reading slows down, context lost, if too much time is spent reading a bilingual dictionary. A more effective alternative: look up only *key* words in a monolingual dictionary.
f	I	See (e) above.
g	E	Attitude may affect reader's ability: if you think that you won't be able to comprehend a text, you probably won't!
h	E	Signals relationship between ideas; stresses text coherence.
i	I	Teacher-dependent tendency developed; reader is lost, later, without teacher.
j	E	Good, because reading strategies vary according to your reading purpose (e.g. in scanning a directory, reader doesn't focus on every detail, only certain features).
k	I	Leads to very intensive, careful reading, when perhaps a summary in plain English might help comprehension more.
l	E	Synonyms, related word forms (e.g. verb and noun of root word) may help reader guess the meaning of an unfamiliar word.
m	E	See (c) above.
n	E	Extensive reading; readers improve most quickly by reading a lot.
o	I	If out of context, not very useful; meaning of words is affected by context.
p	E	Coherence of text becomes clearer.
q	E	Can help orient the reader.
r	E	Skimming helps reader understand gist – see (b); it resembles how we read in real life.
s	I and E	Ineffective: if you concentrate on these and look up everything, you slow reading speed. Effective: if you find key words only and only look those up.
t	E	Pre-reading helps readers predict, look for meaning; interact with text.
u	E	See (e) above.
v	E	Reminder of main ideas; can decide which to look up later.

Reading

TASK 3 Browsing... *(pages 60-61)*   15-20 min

The aim of this task is for trainees to learn about different ways that teachers can go about teaching reading.

Step 1   **I**

Trainees read for new ideas about teaching reading. Add any other suggestions you can think of.

Step 2   **P**

Key to Focus questions:

1 *Liu*   **Activity:** Pre-teaching a few key words
          Aim: To help Ls with difficult words

   Kate **Activity:** Ls discuss the topic of a text
          Aims: To warm Ls up; to motivate Ls to want to read

   Kate **Activity:** Ls brainstorm/predict vocabulary
          Aims: To warm Ls up; to introduce or revise vocabulary

   Kate **Activity:** Ls listen to a passage on a related topic
          Aims: To warm Ls up; to introduce vocabulary and/or topic

2 *a* Answers are individual.
   b Usually, to practise pronunciation.
   c, d Answers are individual.

3 *a* *Kate's quote*
   Model: Pre-reading, while-reading and post-reading

   Xu's quote
   'Traditional' model: Ls read text aloud in turn, class goes over unfamiliar vocabulary and T gives L1 translations, T asks Ls comprehension questions.

   b *Kate's quote*
   Advantages:
   • provides solid preparation, making text more comprehensible
   • integrates other skills with reading
   • can encourage critical thinking skills (e.g. prediction, analysing, synthesising).

   Disadvantages:
   • does not resemble usual testing situation/format, may make timed reading tests more difficult for Ls using this model.

   b *Xu's quote*
   Advantages:
   • encourages guessing meaning from context.

   Disadvantages:
   • no preparation before reading/no orientation
   • purpose of reading not clear from onset
   • in defining difficult vocabulary, switching between L1 and L2 may be difficult for some learners.

4 *a* To give Ls a reason to read; to help Ls to read better; to focus Ls' reading.
   b We do: giving Ls a reason to read helps reading in the classroom to resemble reading in real life, motivates them to read and may help them understand the text better.

5 To help Ls get the overall idea before working on details; once Ls have understood the context, they can better guess the meaning of unfamiliar words or details of the passage. Reading a second time allows Ls to focus on the task, and not to be distracted by trying to understand everything the first time round.

6 *a* Liu: Role-play
   b actively use new vocabulary; integrate speaking; check comprehension

   a Liu: Game
   b actively use new vocabulary

   a Kate: Role-play
   b actively use new vocabulary; integrate speaking; check comprehension

   a Kate: Ls write new ending to a story
   b develop creative writing skills; expand on plot; check understanding of text which came before; predict logical ending

   a Kate: Ls discuss issues in a text
   b integrate listening and speaking; expand understanding of topic; express opinions related to topic

TASK 4 Reader's choice *(pages 62-65)*   25-30 min

The aim of this task is to learn about different reading activity types and their aims.

Explain how to complete the chart using Activity A. This activity illustrates two kinds of reading techniques, paraphrasing and extensive reading, so *A* is written in numbers 6 and 11.

Possible answers:

1 G, H, K; 2 G; 3 C; 4 I; 5 J; 6 A, E; 7 F; 8 J;
9 D, K; 10 D, E, H, I; 11 A; 12 B

Time out, take five

Journal entry: My favourite reading tasks

(page 66)   **I** 10 min

In this task individuals reflect on the techniques and activities explored in this unit and write about their personal preferences.

A reading lesson

TASK 5 Upside down, inside out
(page 66)   40-50 mins

This task aims to get trainees to think about the structure of a reading lesson and to plan a complete reading lesson of their own.

Step 1   **G**

As preparation, copy and cut up the lesson plan (p. T67).

Key:

1 Possible order for lesson: i h j a e g f b c d

2 In this order: *a)* i h j; *b)* a e g f b; *c)* c d

Step 2   **G**

Help trainees in their lesson planning with their chosen texts. They can submit these outlines to you for review. See **Unit 13 Plan of Attack** for more on lesson planning.

Microteaching

TASK 6 You can't judge a book by its cover
(page 67)   40 min (preparation), 60-90 min (for three to four presentations in groups)

The aims of this task are for trainees to teach and experience as learners some while-reading activities.

Step 1   **P**

Remind trainees to limit their activity to ten minutes, including reading time, and to look at the Feedback questions (p. 67) as guidelines for preparation.

Step 2   **G** **M**

Divide the class into groups of six to eight. Each group should appoint a timekeeper. Each pair teaches their ten-minute while-reading activity; the rest of the group are learners. After each presentation, the group should spend ten minutes giving feedback to the teachers, answering the Feedback questions.

Game

TASK 7 If the shoe doesn't fit...
(page 67)   **G**   20-30 min

The aim of this game is to help trainees make spontaneous decisions in order to handle situations that commonly arise in teaching reading. In advance, copy one set of **Situation cards** for each group of trainees (pp. T68-69). Go over the instructions (p. 67), then begin the game. The winner is the one to finish most quickly with the highest number of points; stop after about 20 minutes.

9 DEAR DIARY
Teaching writing

In this unit... trainees learn about teaching writing. Two other units explore topics closely related to this one: part of Unit 5 Warming up deals with pre-writing and Unit 11 Right on! deals with responding to learners' writing.

Writing

TASK 1 To whom it may concern
(page 69)   50-60 min

The aim of this task is for trainees to experience and discuss two different approaches to writing.

Step 1   **G** and **I**

Divide the class into As and Bs. You will need to copy enough **Writing assignments**, page T70. The As do their assignment and the Bs do theirs. They can write in class or at home.

Step 2 **P**

Possible answers to Focus questions (you will think of others):

Assignment A

1 no aim stated: only aim is 'write an essay'.

2 no audience stated; only audience is the trainer.

3 • thought up ideas (reasons)
  • organised them in a written outline.

4 more guidance and preparation before writing, e.g. class discussion, input on vocabulary.

Assignment B

1 aims: to persuade readers of the magazine (other English teachers); to inspire readers to reflect on their own motivation for being in the profession.

2 audience: other English teachers, magazine editor, judges of the competition.

3 • wrote notes about positive aspects of teaching and learning
  • focused on positive aspects and wrote sentences
  • wrote introduction
  • wrote conclusion.

4 • read similar articles
  • see magazine to get idea of type of article required.

Step 3 **G**

Answers to Focus questions 2 and 4 will vary. Possible answers to numbers 1 and 3 follow:

1 *Assignment A*
• pre-writing stage brief and not guided: Ls prompted to think of ideas and then organise their thoughts in note form
• assignment includes three reasons (one per paragraph)
• focus on accuracy: grammar and mechanics stressed
• audience: teacher only; no other mentioned
• no aim specified
• no genre (text type) specified; composition (not a real-life text type) only.

Assignment B
• pre-writing stage extended and guided: Ls are helped through different stages (i.e. initial brainstorming, narrowing content, writing punchy introductory sentence, selecting key reason for body, writing summary statement as conclusion)
• assignment includes only one main reason; fewer points expected as Ls spend more time preparing
• focus on message as well as accuracy
• audience specified: magazine readers
• aim specified: to win a prize
• genre specified: magazine article.

3 *Strengths, Assignment A*
• topic personally relevant
• outline or notes prompt writer to plan and organise ideas
• Ls may enjoy sharing reasons for wanting to teach English.

Weaknesses, Assignment A
• activity not very realistic: aim? reader?
• not much guidance given
• no examples provided
• dominant emphasis on correct form (grammar and mechanics) but no attention to content.

Strengths, Assignment B
• topic personally relevant
• giving a realistic writing activity helps (audience, aim and genre are provided)
• publication of winning entry and prize add to motivation
• preparation helps writing and generates ideas
• example introductory and concluding sentences provided as model
• attention to ideas given: content emphasised.

Weaknesses, Assignment B
• time limit is perhaps too short to account for all the preparation expected
• some Ls may wish to write more, explaining more reasons – assignment B asks for one paragraph only
• no reminder/guidance about language (e.g. grammar, functions, register).

TASK 2 Putting pen to paper *(page 70)* 30-45 min

The aim of this task is for trainees to experience and discuss some aspects of group writing.

Note: For Step 1, you will need several pictures of vacation spots (e.g. postcards, magazine pictures).

Step 1 **G**

To prepare, you can do an example with the whole class first.

1 Give one picture of a vacation spot to each group. Number each picture to make the matching later in the task easier.

2 Give trainees ten minutes to complete their paragraphs.

3 Collect in the pictures and descriptions, display them and then ask trainees to match them.

Step 2

Ask trainees to form new groups to discuss the Focus questions. You can hold a plenary to discuss answers. Among possible answers are:

1 The purpose of each stage:

Stage 1
- to collect together useful vocabulary, perhaps discover unfamiliar words and categorise vocabulary
- to interact, establish ideas for content, and reflect on the topic (describing a place).

Stage 2
- to cooperate, revise and edit, seeing writing as part of a thinking process rather than as only generating an end-product
- to be concise and focused on the activity at hand.

Stage 3
- to read each others' work (and perhaps learn from that)
- to practise skim reading.

2 Pre-writing activity:
- It focused attention on the topic and activity and the vocabulary to use.
- It used words from the pre-writing activity in the descriptions.
- It provided an aim and audience.

3 Post-writing activity:
- Trainees individually write their own description of a place they have visited while on holiday.
- Trainees write fuller, individual articles about their pictures.

4 Answers are individual. Possible answers:
- Numerous ideas and vocabulary are produced.
- Different ways of structuring a piece of writing come out in a group discussion.
- Learners revise their writing as they together create a first draft.
- Mixed ability classes can work well: students learn from each other and interact.
- Teacher dependence is decreased; Ls are encouraged to rely on their own abilities.
- Teacher can be a facilitator and has time to monitor the groups' progress.
- Ls might correct each other's mistakes.

5 Answers will vary. Possible disadvantages:
- Some groups may not work well together; stronger students might dominate weaker ones. (Solution: T selects groups who will work well together.)
- Some students may not stay focused on the activity. (Solutions: T can monitor groups actively, remind them of their goal and their responsibility to generate a piece of writing within time limit. T can ask them all to write, so everyone has to produce a piece of writing.)

6 Examples of group writing in real life:
- writing articles (e.g. team of researchers)
- writing a report (e.g. social workers describe a client)
- writing a proposal or a plan (e.g. to win a government grant)
- writing a brochure (e.g. to inform about a company or a course).

Aims of real-life group writing:
- to pool ideas or experience
- to use different people's skills (e.g. expertise, ability to write copy) collectively to the best advantage
- to save time later with others rejecting the final copy
- to involve people.

Analysing writing activities

TASK 3 Doodling *(pages 70-72)* 50-60 min

The aims of this task are for trainees to analyse six writing activities and to create pre- and post-writing activities for them.

Step 1

Answers to the questions will vary. For question 3, generally speaking, in real life we do have an aim, audience, and genre in mind when we write.

Step 2

Make sure that all trainees understand the example before beginning work; if necessary, supply another example of your own. Here are some possible answers:

A *aim:* to explain
audience: parents
genre: school report
level: low-intermediate

B *aim:* to obtain information
audience: Cyclorama Holidays or Windmill Hill Place Tennis Resort
genre: formal/business letter
level: intermediate

C *aim:* to describe someone from another person's viewpoint
audience: Mary Shelley's daughter
genre: unclear
level: high-beginner/low-intermediate and above

D *aim:* invite/persuade someone
audience: friend
genre: informal letter
level: high-beginning and above

E *aim:* to persuade
  audience: peers
  genre: radio advertisement
  level: intermediate or above

F *aim:* to describe people
  audience: teenagers
  genre: magazine article
  level: low-intermediate and above

Step 3

Trainees' suggestions for pre-writing and post-writing activities will vary. In reviewing them, make sure that the overall aims of their activities are clear and that the pre-writing activity would help prepare learners to write and the post-writing activity to consolidate what was written. Some suggestions:

1 Pre-writing

Writing activity A
Ls read statements about the contents of Rosie's report and have to indicate whether they are True or False.

Writing activity B
Ls read an advertisement for a study holiday and a letter that someone wrote to the holiday centre. Ls have to find out things about the letter that show it is formal.

Writing activity C
Ls listen to a tape about Mary Shelley and note down the answers to some questions (e.g. *When and where was Mary born? Who was her husband?*).

Writing activity D
Ls write sentences about what a friend is going to do this weekend, using these ideas: go skiing; play basketball; visit a museum; study Maths; etc.

Writing activity E
Ls listen to a radio advertisement for the Gateway Holidays European Cities tour.

Writing activity F
Ls listen to a tape: foreign learners are interviewed about the lives of teenagers in their countries. Ls listen and make notes about what their parents let them do, make them do, and want them to do.

2 Post-writing

Writing activity A
Ls ask each other ten questions about their performance at school (e.g. *Have you worked hard in (history) this year? Is your handwriting tidy? Are you ever late for class?*). Ls then write each other's reports.

Writing activity B
Partners reply in writing to letter sent as if they are working at the holiday centre. Role-play in small groups: decide which holiday you want to take and why, based on the replies from adverts.

Writing activity C
Role-play: Mary Shelley's daughter describes her mother to a friend; T provides some prompt questions to aid discussion.

Writing activity D
Role-play: telephone call between you and friend. Friend rings up to accept your invitation; you have to decide where to meet, when, etc.

Writing activity E
Ls listen to some of the radio adverts that their classmates have written and ask further questions about the tour (e.g. *How will we travel? How many countries will we visit?*)

Writing activity F
Role-play: Ls pretend they are teenagers from another country and have to persuade others in their group that their life is the best.

TASK 4 A stroke of the pen *(page 73)*   25-30 min

The aim of this task is for trainees to adapt writing activities to make them more communicative.

Step 1

Answers to stage 2 will vary. Here are two examples:

Topic: Study holidays

Activity: Write an editorial essay which will appear on the Opinion Page of your school newspaper. State your opinion for or against the proposed holidays beginning two weeks later.
Aim: to persuade someone
Audience: fellow learners
Genre: editorial/ opinion page/school newspaper

Topic: A school sports day

Activity: You are a reporter for your school magazine. Write a short but lively article about one sporting event at the recent school sports day.
Aim: to describe a sporting event
Audience: fellow learners
Genre: school magazine article

Step 2

You may wish to put up all the activities on the wall to help trainees read others' work. Allow time for class discussion.

Time out, take five

Journal entry: Where do I stand now?
(page 73) 10 min

In this journal entry, trainees reflect on the degree to which they feel prepared to teach writing. Issues related to responding to writing are addressed in **Unit 11 Right on!**

Microteaching

TASK 5 Take note
(page 74) 40-50 min (excluding preparation time)

The aim of this task is for trainees to create and experience pre-writing and post-writing activities.

Step 1

Clarify the answers to question 1 before trainees move on to question 2:

aim: to tell someone how to make a sandwich
audience: readers of a cookery book
genre: recipe
level: intermediate

Step 2

Microteaching: Ask two or four pairs to teach the whole class. After each presentation, spend ten minutes giving feedback to the presenters, answering the Feedback questions.

Game

TASK 6 Writer's block
(page 74) 25-30 min

In this game, trainees match problems in teaching writing to possible solutions. You will need to copy and cut up sets of **Problem cards** (p. T71) and **Solution cards** (p. T72) in preparation.

Go over the instructions (p. 74). Explain that when they draw a **Wild card**, trainees must come up with a writing problem and a solution on their own; to help the trainees, you may wish to prepare a few suggestions for **Wild cards** that characterise your teaching context. After 20 minutes or when all the problems have been solved, hold a plenary to confirm the correct answers, listed below. Discuss any additional solutions you or the trainees suggest. Possible answers (these are our preferred solutions; you may disagree):

1 b, j	8 k	15 c	22 a
2 b, j	9 s	16 x	23 w
3 l	10 e, f	17 q	24 v
4 d, l	11 b	18 g	25 u
5 n	12 d	19 d	26 y
6 h	13 o	20 z	
7 t	14 i	21 p	

10 PUTTING IT ALL TOGETHER
Integrating the skills

In this unit... trainees learn how to integrate language skills (listening, speaking, reading, and writing), grammar and vocabulary into unified lessons. This unit builds on the work of Unit 5 Warming up, and on those units related to teaching individual language areas: Unit 3 Grasping grammar, Unit 4 How do you do?, Unit 6 Now hear this, Unit 7 Speaking your mind, Unit 8 Between the lines, and Unit 9 Dear diary.

Reflection

TASK 1 Warp and weft *(pages 76-77)* 10-20 min

The aim of this task is to raise awareness about the interrelatedness of language skills in real life and in the classroom.

Step 1 **P**

Key: a) 7; b) 9; c) 3; d) 5; e) 2; f) 4; g) 6; h) 1
(8 and 10 are distractors).

Step 2

Some possible answers are:

1 Post-listening activities:

- Role-play the next conversation that these people have (speaking).
- Write invitations to people (writing).
- Call the hostess and express your regrets about not coming to the party (speaking).
- Read a partially completed shopping list for the party; add any forgotten items (reading/writing).

2 Pre-listening activities:

Imagine you are meeting some friends and you are going to discuss your New Year's Eve party.
- Make a list of topics you will discuss with them (writing).
- Look over several ads for nightclubs and discos that hold New Year's Eve parties and decide which you want to go to (reading).
- Write a list of your top three favourite activities for New Year's Eve, then discuss them with others (writing/speaking).

An integrated skills lesson

TASK 2 In unison *(page 77)*   30-45 min

This task aims to work on an integrated skills lesson plan. In advance, photocopy and cut up the plan on page T73. Make one set for every pair of trainees.

Step 1   **P**

One possible order:

1 i; 2 e; 3 h; 4 d; 5 a; 6 g; 7 c; 8 f; 9 b

Step 2   **G**

Possible answers to the Focus questions are:

1 Answers may vary.

   a Another possible order is:
   1 e; 2 i; 3 d; 4 h; 5 a; 6 g; 7 c; 8 f; 9 b.
   b The effect would be minimally different: Ls would receive an orientation to the project before doing group work. Could be beneficial for classes where Ls are easily distracted in group work.

2, 3 Answers are individual.

4 Answers will vary. Sample answers are:
- Ls illustrate their posters with drawings or pictures of things that are personally meaningful to each learner (e.g. pet dog).
- Ls read a few sentences about some of the famous people they have illustrated their posters with.
- Ls add a speech bubble onto the poster that the famous people might say.
- Ls find a picture of a famous person that they like and write a 3-sentence paragraph about them.

5 Answers are individual.

TASK 3 There's a song in my heart
(pages 78-79)   40-45 min

The purpose of this task is to provide a sample integrated skills lesson for integrating skills based on a song which trainees analyse.

Possible answers to the Focus questions are:

1 Intermediate level – see vocabulary.

2 *a* Grammar is not directly taught.
  b Effect of omission: focus of the lesson is on meaning and communication rather than on grammar. Increased fluency may be the end result.

3 Some advantages are:
- Materials may be motivating – topic/singer of interest.
- Cultural aspect of an English-speaking country is learnt.
- Appeals to auditory learners especially well.
- May be an entertaining way to learn.

4 Some disadvantages are:
- Materials may be more complex and richer than prepared materials in a coursebook.
- Materials may intimidate learners who are used to being encouraged to understand every single word.

5 Steps in the lesson are clearly linked and recycle the same language.

6 Answers are individual.

Time out, take five

**Journal entry: Which language
areas do I prefer?** *(page 79)*   10 min

In this journal trainees reflect on which language areas they prefer practising as learners and which they might prefer teaching, and why.

Integrated skills activities

TASK 4 Kaleidoscope *(pages 80-81)*   40-45 min

This task aims to demonstrate ways to use a reading passage as a basis for other skills area work.

Step 1

Answers to questions will vary according to your teaching context.

Step 2 **G**

Trainees form new groups of four to discuss their answers. Possible answers are:

1 Aims of each integrated skills activity:

A Develop vocabulary.
B Consolidate understanding of text; practise narrative form of writing.
C Practise with question formation (word order, etc.); additional perspective on story.
D Grasp main ideas from reading.
E Practise writing conclusions.
F Confirmation of story; check understanding of reading for details.
G Practise present tenses.
H Practise realistic oral communication: two-way interaction with others.
I Grasp specific details.
J Practise recognising irregular verb forms; rehearse 3 verb forms (infinitive, irregular simple past, past participle).

2 *a* Answers will vary. Possible answers are: A, B, H.
   b Answers are individual.

Lesson planning and microteaching

TASK 5 **A unified vision** *(pages 81-82)*   90 min
(45 min for planning, 45 min for teaching)

The aim of the task is for trainees to design an integrated skills lesson and to experience part of it in a microteaching activity.

If the trainees have never written a lesson plan before, go over the task instructions more carefully and possibly direct the trainees to **Unit 13 Plan of attack.**

Step 1 **P**

Alternative: Trainees write their own profile of learners.

Step 2 **G**

Hold a plenary where groups report on the strengths of their lesson plans before microteaching from them.

Step 3 **G**

Pick two groups of trainees to teach their activities, or more if you have time. The others in their group observe the microteaching, take notes on how it goes and join in the feedback.

Step 4 **G** and **C** and **M**

Allow ten minutes per microteaching, and up to ten minutes for feedback. Encourage supportive feedback prompted by the Feedback questions (p. 82).

11 RIGHT ON!
Responding to learners' writing

In this unit... trainees learn about and practise responding to learners' writing, focusing on content and organisation, identifying strengths and weaknesses. It is closely related to Unit 9 Dear diary (pp. 69-75) on teaching writing and Unit 12 We all make mistakes (pp. 92-97) on dealing with errors in speaking. For definitions of the words *error* and *mistake*, see page 93.

Reflection

TASK 1 **'Responding' means...**
(pages 83-84)   15-20 min

The aim of this task is to define 'responding' and perhaps to expand the trainees' definition of responding to learner writing.

Step 1

You can complete this questionnaire yourself and share your responses with the trainees in a plenary as a follow-on to Step 2.

Step 2

Hold a plenary afterwards and encourage diverse answers.

TASK 2 Taking the plunge *(pages 84-85)* 25-30 min

The aim of this task is to discover how trainees would now respond to learners' written work. You will need to provide a copy of Henny's story (p. T74) for each trainee.

Step 1

Clarify the **Profile of the learner: Henny** and **Henny's writing task** (p. 84) and ask trainees to think about question 3 before they respond to Henny's writing in question 4. Emphasise that trainees should write directly on Henny's work, as if they were his teacher.

Step 2 **G**

Trainees' answers will vary.

Possible answers to the Focus questions:

1
a
- Ask Henny to write several drafts of the story.
- Ask probing questions about the content to get him to write more.
- De-emphasise error correction unless the errors interfere a lot with communication.

b
- Tell Henny his most characteristic errors.
- Indicate his errors and show him the correct form.
- Provide further explanation and exercises about his typical errors.
- Develop peer- and self-correction exercises to help Henny to monitor his own and others' writing for errors.

2 *a* and *b* Marks and the reasons for marks will vary.

c
- Henny has a standard against which to measure future progress.
- The teacher can keep a record of Henny's marks and measure his progress and ability.

d
- Henny may be discouraged if the mark is lower than he expected.
- Henny may not pay attention to the teacher's comments, but focus on the mark he received.

Responding

TASK 3 If u kn rd this... *(pages 85-86)* 20-35 min

The aims of this task are to learn about using symbols to give feedback on written work and to reflect on the value of using them. You might like to give trainees a clean copy of Henny's story (page T74) to use here.

Step 1

As preparation, you can make your own list of symbols for giving learners feedback on their writing. Save this list for use in Step 2.

Step 2

Hold a plenary to check answers. See below for the answer key.

Step 3

Hold a plenary to discuss which errors might be indicated.

SYMBOL	EXPLANATION	EXAMPLE
S	spelling error	*Haus; holyday*
P	punctuation error	*Haus* (should be *house.*)
V	verb tense error	*was dead*; various other forms of passive voice incorrect (e.g. *is not yet found, murdered with a book*)
WO	incorrect word order	*is yet not found*
WW	wrong word used	*face* (should be *head*)
Agr	agreement (subject-verb, adjective-noun or noun-pronoun)	*two month; the police has*
//	new paragraph needed	Possible new paragraph at *The woman probably murdered...*
R-O	run-on sentence	Line 1: *...in her Haus probably she...*; Lines 3-4: *... murdered with a book she was hit*
∧	something's missing	*Yesterday old woman; The woman probably murdered*
☺	good; well done; I like this	good use of colourful vocabulary (*murdered, clues, eye witnesses, shabby, seedy*)
?	I don't understand this	—

34 TRAINER'S NOTES

Step 4 **G**

Trainees work in groups and compare how they marked Henny's story, discussing the Focus questions.

1 Answers will vary.

2 Answers will vary. We would indicate errors which interfere with understanding first, underline them and in some cases indicate the type of error by using a correction symbol in the margin. However, we would indicate a limited number of errors since learners can only absorb a few pieces of information at one time.

3 Answers will vary. We would say that run-on sentence errors are the most important type in this example, as they confuse the reader the most. We would ignore Henny's passive voice errors since he has not yet been taught that tense.

4 We believe that it is important to give positive feedback, so that learners do not feel discouraged by their errors. Focusing on what they do right can motivate learners to write more and to experiment with language.

5 Answers will vary; we hope that trainees are expanding their idea of what responding to writing means by this stage in the unit.

TASK 4 A bird's eye view *(pages 86-87)*   20-35 min

The aim of this task is learn to respond to the organisation and contents of a piece of writing.

Step 1 **C**

Clarify the **Profile of the learner: Margareta** and **Margareta's writing task**.

Step 2

Check answers in a brief plenary discussion. Answers will vary; accept all that seem reasonable. Some possible answers are:

1 Main ideas in Margareta's letter (p. T75):
- My opinion about a successful life.
- Some people consider a successful life to be a happy family.
- Some people consider a successful life to do with work.
- Poor people consider a successful life to be in getting small things.
- Sportsmen consider winning to be part of a successful life.

2
- 1st paragraph: 1 main idea
- 2nd paragraph: 4 main ideas
- 3rd, 4th, 5th, 6th paragraphs: 1 main idea each
- 7th paragraph: 1 idea (closing, greeting)

3 *a* One main idea supported by insufficient detail: what a successful life is for a sportsman. (You will have more details for other main ideas.)
b Extra information Margareta might add to support her main idea about sportsmen: some examples of famous sports figures and comments about how their lives are successful. (You will have different ideas for expanding on other main ideas.)

Step 3

Responses to Margareta's letter will be individual. Here is one possible response:

> Margareta – You have several good ideas here, but too many of them are in the same paragraph. Make sure you only have one main idea for each paragraph. Make sure, too, that each main idea is supported by sufficient details. You could give some real examples here, for example about sportsmen or about yourself.

Step 4

Answers will vary. Have a brief plenary to hear some of the preferred responses. We believe that responses with very specific ideas for improvement are helpful.

TASK 5 Tips from teachers
(pages 87-88)   **G**   20-25 min

The aim of this task is to develop trainees' awareness of ways to respond to errors by reading the opinions of experienced teachers. Allow 10-15 minutes for group discussion of the Focus questions. Possible answers are:

1 Answers will be individual.

2 *a* Beginners: Bartholomew and Frank.
Ls are just starting out in English and may need more encouragement and motivation to write.
b Advanced classes: all quotes promoting self-correction and peer editing (e.g. Doreen, Eve and Ishmael).

3 Perhaps Frank and Guus (time-consuming).

4 For teenagers: Johan, Ishmael and Kala. For adults: Bartholomew.

TASK 6 Bravo! *(page 89)*   20-25 min

The aims of this task are to help trainees recognise the strengths of learners' writing and to practise giving encouraging feedback.

Step 1

You will need to copy **Margareta's letter** on page T75 for your trainees.

Hold a plenary to discuss answers. Possible answers are:

a **Content**
- Lots of colourful images help the reader picture success.
- The reader understands that the definition of success depends on the individual.

b **Organisation**
- Basic structure is logical: introductory statement, body of examples, and conclusion.
- Margareta has written a piece that looks like a letter.

c **Grammar**
- Good use of present tense for general truths.
- Good self-correction of 'people' to 'person'.

Step 2

Encourage trainees to mention specific points (e.g. *Lots of colourful images help your reader really picture success*) rather than make vague positive comments (e.g. *Good job!*).

Step 3 **P**

As a follow-on to the pair work, ask for a show of hands to find out how many people wrote general comments (like *Very good* or *Well done*) and how many wrote more specific ones. Discuss the effects of different types of feedback.

Time out, take five

Journal entry: On the receiving end
(page 89) 10 min

In this journal entry, trainees reflect on their personal experience as learners in receiving feedback on their writing.

Using journals

TASK 7 Very truly yours *(pages 89-90)*   45-50 min

The aim of this task is to introduce and experience dialogue journal writing in the classroom. You will need one copy of the journals on page T76 per trainee for Step 2.

Step 1

Collate the information in this brainstorm on the board. A few examples:

Dialogue Journals

Who?
- L writes to L
- L writes to T and then T to L
- trainer and trainee write to each other
- trainees write to each other in pairs.

What?
- topics Ls are interested in
- issues related to class
- anything that gets Ls writing!

Where?
- in the classroom
- in the library at school
- at home.

When?
- at the beginning or end of class
- in the middle of class, as a break between activities
- once or twice a week
- every day
- once a week.

How?
- exchanged between Ls (or trainees) in the same class
- exchanged between Ls in different classes
- exchanged between T and Ls
- exchanged between trainer and trainees
- using a notebook: writer writes on one page, reader responds on the opposite page
- writing via electronic mail messages.

Why?
- to encourage fluency in writing
- to increase self-confidence in writing
- to get feedback on classroom activities
- to reduce writer's block.

Step 2

Trainees work in pairs and analyse two journal entries. Answers to the questions are:

CATALINA'S JOURNAL

- *Level of L:* beginner
- *Age of L:* probably primary school, maybe 10 yrs old
- *Subject:* personal anecdote about a cat
- *Example language problem:* no distinction in verb tenses (all present)
- *Visuals included:* yes
- *If so, whose?* child's own drawing
- *What does 'mone' probably mean?* 'morning' or 'Monday'
- *Nature of teacher's reply:*
  content: agrees it was a sad experience
  tone of reply: sympathetic

MIGUEL'S JOURNAL

- *Level:* Beginner
- *Age:* 12
- *Subject:* Barcroft school and school in home country (El Salvador)
- *Example language problem:* no end to sentences – run-on sentences
- *Visuals included:* no
- *What does 'pleople' probably mean?* 'people'
- *What other types of errors does Miguel make?* spelling, verb tense, capitalisation, run-on sentences

36 TRAINER'S NOTES

- *Nature of teacher's reply:*
  content: T writes about school subjects L studies; T summarises
  tone of reply: friendly
  use of L1: helps Miguel build vocabulary by translating
  length of sentences: short simple sentences model a correct sentence form

Step 3   ▮

Share some trainees' responses and their reasons for their choice of response. For comparison's sake, here is the actual teacher's reply to Elizabeth's journal:

> *That is a serious problem. Have you discussed it with your Mother? If she knows the people involved she may have an idea. If it is someone here at school, someone your Mother doesn't know well, you would be wise to tell Mrs. F. Running away is an extremely dangerous thing to do. I hope you see that they get help.[1]*

Step 4   **G**

1

CATALINA	MIGUEL	ELIZABETH
a No.	*a* No.	
b Yes – responds in sympathetic way.	*b* Yes – summarises ideas; answers his questions; asks further questions.	Answers will be individual, according to the trainees' responses to Elizabeth.
c Yes. T asks if Catalina cried when she saw the little cat.	*c* Yes. T asks Miguel to expand on his comments about school in El Salvador.	

2 We would not mark these except perhaps giving points for handing the journals in and keeping up with them. The idea of writing journals is to encourage the learners to write freely, without worrying about errors or marks.

3 Some sample topics:
- pop music
- pets
- fashion
- famous athletes
- adventure
- TV shows
- movie stars
- space exploration
- hobbies

[1] Peyton and Reed (1990).

4 Large classes: Ls write to other Ls, within same class or to another class (same level, slightly lower or higher). T collects and reads journals every so often, or Ls submit their best entry or the one they want their T to read. Exchange could be weekly or bi-weekly; entries could be daily or several times a week.

5 Beginners:
- Begin once Ls have learned some spoken English.
- Encourage any type of journal entry – word, short sentences, illustrations, quotes, etc.
- Encourage Ls to illustrate journals with pictures or photos.

6 For Ls, advantages are:
- They write for a real purpose and a real audience.
- Ls receive interesting and genuine response.
- Ls express ideas that are important to them.
- Writing journals may help reduce 'writer's block'.
- Ls may become more fluent writers.

For T, advantages are:
- Using journals increases communication with Ls, if T reads and responds to the journals.
- T can individualise language learning.
- T can obtain useful information for future lessons.
- T can motivate Ls to read and write more.

Homework

TASK 8 Tackling it yourself *(page 90)*   20-30 min

The aim of this task is to consolidate what has been learnt in this unit. You may wish trainees to exchange their completed responses before handing them in to you to evaluate.

Step 1   ▮

You will need to provide copies of **Tackling it yourself** (p. T77) for your trainees. Clarify the **Profile of the learner: Jan** and **Jan's writing task**.

Step 2   ▮

Ask trainees to limit themselves to 15 minutes when responding to this piece of writing, thus simulating a real situation. Remind them of the different ways of responding to writing that they dealt with in this unit.

Alternative: This could be done outside class, if trainees respect the time limit.

Step 3   ▮

You can hold a plenary to find out how trainees answered the follow-up questions, particularly question 7.

12 WE ALL MAKE MISTAKES
Dealing with spoken errors

In this unit... trainees reflect on spoken mistakes and errors and learn how to manage them in the classroom. It relates to Unit 7 Speaking your mind about teaching speaking and Unit 11 Right on! about responding to writing.

Reflection

TASK 1 Look where you're going!
(pages 92-93) 15-20 min

This task aims to raise the trainees' awareness of the role that mistakes play in learning.

Step 1 **I**

Responses to the questions are individual.

Step 2 **G**

Hold a plenary discussion about trainees' responses.

Step 3 **I**

Briefly discuss the trainees' views about the text.

What are errors and mistakes?

TASK 2 Was it an error or a mistake?
(pages 93-94) 5-10 min

The aim of this task is to clarify the difference between an error and a mistake.

Step 1 **I**

The **Dictionary definition** and the **Reading: Errors and mistakes** (p. 93) show the common distinction made by some linguists between an *error* and a *mistake*, and leads into Step 2.

Step 2 **I** and **G**

Check trainees' responses to the questions in plenary. It is sometimes difficult to know whether something is an error or a mistake. For example, a learner who says *I goed** to school* instead of *I went to school* might be over-generalising but also be aware of the correct form; he has forgotten and just needs reminding of it.

TASK 3 Don't make a fool of yourself
(page 94) **P** and **G** and **C** 20-30 min

The aim of this task is to think about typical English language errors and their possible causes. Some possible responses to the questions:

1 and 2 Typical English errors vary according to first language.

3 Some possible causes of errors:

- Learners are tired or careless and just forget the correct language (= a mistake).
- The influence of the first language on learning a second language; for example, a Polish or a Chinese learner might say *I am going to States** in summer*** instead of *I'm going to <u>the</u> States in <u>the</u> summer* because Polish and Chinese both lack articles.
- Learners know a rule, but haven't processed the language deeply enough for it to have become automatic.
- Learners know a rule, but over-generalise; for example, they know the regular past tense is made by adding *-ed* to the infinitive, so might create a sentence such as *She comed** to my party* instead of *She came to my party*.
- Learners know they are not correct, but are trying to communicate something quite complicated by using the language they already know.

Observation

TASK 4 Whoops! *(pages 94-95)* 45-60 min

The aims of this observation task are to observe how a teacher deals with spoken errors and for trainees to decide how to correct errors as teachers.

Step 1 **I**

Clarify the observation task. Trainees will each need a copy of the **Observation table: Spoken errors** on page T78.

Step 2 **I**

Collect in trainees' written answers to the Post-observation questions or discuss them in class.

Correcting in class

TASK 5 Erroroleplay *(page 95)* 45-60 min

This task aims to raise and discuss issues about dealing with errors and mistakes, by experiencing a role-play where four teachers deal with errors and mistakes in different ways.

During the *Erroroleplay*, trainees experience four different teachers teaching them; each of the 'teachers' has a separate task to teach and a different error correction style. This task is complex, but once it gets going, it runs itself. The teachers who trainees role-play are caricatures; most teachers are a mixture of all four. You will need to prepare copies of the material accompanying this task in advance (pp. T79-82).

Step 1

Instructions

1 Select four trainees to play the four teacher roles and give each one of them a role card (pp. T79-81).

All four 'teachers' have the following tasks:

a to set up their activity;
b to play a role, using a particular error-correction strategy.

Here is a brief description of the four teacher roles:

The four teacher roles

Ms/Mr Aloof (p. T79)
ignores the group and corrects no errors.

Ms/Mr Zeal (p. T80)
joins the group so enthusiastically that s/he forgets to correct errors.

Ms/Mr Busybody (p. T80 and pp. T81-82)
continually intervenes, immediately correcting any learner who makes an error.

Ms/Mr Eavesdrop (p. T81)
monitors the activity, writes down any errors made and gives language feedback at the end of the task.

2 Divide the class into **four** small groups which cannot overhear each other.

3 Give one trainee in each small group the learner role: Ms/Mr Catnap role card (p. T81). These trainees play learners who have problems in spoken English throughout the role-play. Choose trainees who you think can play this role with enthusiasm and who do not mind making errors in front of peers.

4 The role-play begins. Each teacher teaches their first group for ten minutes.

5 Immediately after each activity, give the trainees time to answer the questions (p. 95) in groups.

6 The role-playing teachers rotate, moving to the next group, setting up the same task with their new group and playing the same role. After each task, again give the trainees time to answer the questions on page 95. Repeat until each group has experienced all four teachers.

Step 2

Discuss your trainees' answers in plenary. Some possible responses:

1 Teachers should interrupt learners when they make a mistake or error when...
- they want learners to be accurate, for example when presenting a new structure and learners are practising it for the first time.
- the main aim of a group task is practising something and learners are constantly wrong. For example, if you are practising past tense questions and a majority of learners in a group is consistently making the same error, *Did he comes** on Saturday?*, you might stop the group work and remind the whole class of the correct form.

2 Teachers can give delayed feedback in the following situation: ...
- if learners are in the middle of an activity (e.g. role-play or a group discussion); you can make a note of errors and wait until the activity is finished to correct them (here, fluency and effective communication are aims).

3 Some errors or mistakes should remain uncorrected by the teacher, for example...
- in the middle of a role-play or group work.
- if a shy or not very strong learner is daring to communicate.
- if a learner is trying to express a complex idea.
- if a learner is trying to express something of personal significance or emotional content: the message is more important than correct English.

4 Teachers can correct learners in different ways according to the type of tasks which they do, for example...
- during fluency activities, errors are not ignored totally: you can monitor a group or pair work activity, making a note of common errors to return to.
- if the aim is accuracy, a teacher might correct more frequently.

5 Teachers can vary their error correction strategies according to learners' personalities, by...
- correcting shy learners less, and encouraging them to communicate.
- correcting stronger Ls more, so they are challenged.

6 Teachers can help learners to self-correct or to correct each other's spoken errors by...
- making a gesture, stopping the learner, giving a questioning look or saying *Er...?* The learner then tries to say the correct thing.
- indicating the nature of the error, by saying, for example, *Past tense*.

- stressing the incorrect form to indicate where the error is: *He GOED** to Moscow?*
- repeating the sentence up to where the error was made and then leaving a gap for the learner to provide the correction. For example, a learner says *I went at** school* and the teacher says, *I went...?*
- repeating the sentence with a questioning intonation, indicating there is a error somewhere: *'I went at** school?'*
- asking the whole class for the correct form.
- asking another learner for a correct response and then asking the learner who made the error to repeat the correct form.
- writing the incorrect language on the blackboard and asking the learners to think of the correct form.
- asking a learner to write down errors made and correct them at the end of the activity.

7 Some advantages of self-correction and peer correction:
- The teacher learns how much her learners do and do not know.
- Learners really listen more to each other and understand they can learn from each other.
- Learners might begin to correct each other independently in group and/or pair work if the teacher encourages peer correction in whole-class activities.
- Learners feel more confident and independent.
- Learners discover they do know the right answer.

8 Some disadvantages of self-correction and peer correction:
- Some learners might feel superior to others.
- Some learners in some cultures are not used to criticising each other.
- The same two or three people might always answer.
- The learner who is corrected might feel embarrassed and not contribute so well in future classes.

9 Five practical ways of giving feedback on spoken errors:
- The teacher writes down individual learners' errors on a small piece of paper and hands each learner their own errors and the corrections.
- The teacher gives an explanation about why something is wrong.
- Observers are used (for example, in group work) who write down errors and give feedback later.
- The teacher says gently *That was wrong; it should be...*
- The teacher tells the learner the correct answer.
- The teacher monitors group or pair work, making a note of incorrect sentences or words and then gives feedback after the activity is over, either orally or by writing the errors on the board and asking for the corrections.
- The teacher prepares a remedial lesson on problems which are common to many members of the group.
- The teacher writes the errors on the board; the class corrects them together, or corrects them in pairs or groups.

- The teacher prepares a worksheet on errors for next lesson.

10 Answers are individual.

Afterwards, have a plenary discussion about important issues that came up in Step 2.

TASK 6 What I would do
(page 96)   20-30 min

This activity aims to see how far trainees can now decide on error correction techniques for spoken errors and mistakes. Some suggested answers:

1 *a* Repeat the sentence, with a questioning intonation, emphasising *Have you ever WENT?*, thus indicating where the error is.
b Give a short explanation about the difference between the past and present perfect tenses (if we know where, then it would be the past tense) and ask the learner the question again.
c Ask another learner, elicit the correct answer; return to the first learner who made the error and ask him to repeat the correct answer.

2 *a* Ask learners, *I am GO?* to see if they can self-correct.
b Remind learners of the difference between the present simple and continuous tenses.

3 *a* Ask another learner, elicit the correct answer and return to the first learner who might be able to self-correct.
b Do not correct at all: the aim is to discuss the trip, not grammar. Return to *let's* at another time.
c Say yourself, *Let's go swimming* and hope the learner hears and remembers the correct form.

4 *a* Ask the learner, *How old is she?* and hope the learner can self-correct.
b Say with rising intonation, *Three and seventy?* and hope the learner can self-correct.
c Ask the class, *Is that right, three and seventy?* and hope another learner corrects the error.

5 *a* Pick up another object, belonging to a male learner, and say, *They're his*; ask first learner again, *Whose keys are these?* and hope the learner can self-correct.
b Ask the learner with rising intonation, *They're him?* thus indicating an error; try to elicit correct answer.
c Say gently, *They're HIS* and ask learner to repeat after you.

6 *a* Stop the class working and remind them to use, *We are going...*
b Go around each group, reminding them to use, *We are going...*
c Do a revision lesson next time on *We are going*; leave the error this time.

7 Similar answers to situation 5.

40 ◆ TRAINER'S NOTES

8 *a* At the end of the reading, ask whole class to repeat *ready* and *happened* in chorus.
   b Ask some Ls to repeat the words individually.

9 Similar answers to situation 5.

10 *a* Ignore the error; the aim of the activity is communication.
   b Say, *You want to go to the Chinese restaurant, do you?* and hope the learner hears and remembers the correct form.

Time out, take five

Journal entry: My beliefs about errors
(page 97)   **I** 10 min

In this task, trainees reflect on their beliefs about mistakes and errors.

13 PLAN OF ATTACK
Lesson planning

In this unit... trainees evaluate, improve and produce lesson plans.

Lesson plans

TASK 1 Bits and pieces *(pages 98-99)*   20 min

The aim of this task is to decide which are important elements to include in a lesson plan.

Steps 1 and 2   **I** and **P**

Emphasise that trainees should talk about a learning experience outside English language teaching.

Step 3   **G**

Hold a brief plenary to discuss trainees' conclusions.

TASK 2 My blueprint *(pages 99-100)*   **I** 10 min

Hold a plenary discussion about issues raised here.

Observation

TASK 3 Deduce the lesson plan
(page 100)   40-50 min (excluding observation)

This observation task aims to put the trainees in the place of learners, who are normally unaware of the lesson plan that a teacher uses, by guiding them to guess the lesson plan of the teacher they are observing.

Step 1   **I** or **P**

Trainees each need a copy of the **Observation table: Deduce the lesson plan** on page T83; alternatively, they can write their own plan.

Step 2   **I** or **P**

If trainees do the observation task in pairs, they can discuss the Post-observation questions and write their answers together.

Alternatives: If trainees cannot observe a lesson, they could deduce the lesson plan of one of your training sessions or use the Lesson Transcript on page T50.

Lesson plans

TASK 4 Topsy-turvy *(page 101)*   **G** 30 min

The aim of this activity is to raise awareness of how different stages of a lesson fit together. Photocopy the jumbled lesson plan on page T84 and cut up the stages into strips for each group.

Key

1 Possible order of lesson plan: g, c, b, d, h, e, f, a. There are other possibilities.

2 A possible next stage of the lesson: learners write a letter to a foreign penfriend about their own typical Sunday, saying what they do and don't do.

Aims

TASK 5 Aim straight *(page 102)*   20-30 min

The aim of this task is to learn about different types of aims. You need to have done **Task 4 Topsy-turvy** in order to do this task.

Step 1   **G**

Key: 1 –; 2 –; 3 h, e; 4 a; 5 f, b, d; 6 b, e; 7 d

Step 2 P

In our experience, it is difficult for trainees to state specific aims for activities as well as general aims for lessons. In Step 2, they match types of aims with the aims in Step 1.

Key: (you may disagree!)

Topic aims: 7, 3
Grammar aims: 1, 5
Communication aims: perhaps 5, 6 and 7
Vocabulary aims: 6
Function aims: 7
Skill aims: 4, 5, maybe 2
Pronunciation aims: —
Group dynamics aims: —
Reviewing aims: 5, 6
Cultural aims: 7
Organisational aims: —

Follow-on: Find some tasks in coursebooks so trainees can decide what their aims are.

Evaluating a plan

TASK 6 Face lift *(pages 103-104)*   20-30 min

The aim of this task is to evaluate a lesson plan written by a teacher trainee.

Step 1 P

Key:

1 Yes, she introduces different professions. However, the aims could be more specific and extensive.

2 Additional aims: practising present simple tense questions and answers; writing about the future.

3 T could try to elicit names of some professions.

4 There is rather a lot of mime; we would keep the mime at the oral practice stage but omit it elsewhere and replace it with something else.

5 They aren't really linked together. There is no link between stage 4 and the rest of the lesson and there is no clear link between stage 1 and stages 2 and 3.

6 Omit the writing; omit the review stage (b) (confusion could arise between the simple present and present continuous tenses); a link can be made between present simple revision and what professionals do every day.

7 Perhaps add a column in the plan to show where Ls are working in pairs, groups or individually.

8 It isn't!

9 We would omit the writing activity and replace it with one related to the lesson aims, e.g. a guessing game: learners write ten sentences down about a profession in the present simple tense (Example: *A vet. He works outside, he works with animals, he has good qualifications,* etc.); the learners read out their sentences and others then guess the profession.

10 T could elicit more from the learners throughout and involve them more. See suggestions above.

Step 2 P

Organise circulation around the class of the new lesson plans.

Game

TASK 7 Lesson planning snakes
and ladders *(page 105)*   G 20 min

The aim of this game is to practise reacting to unforeseen circumstances in lessons. Each group will need one set of materials (pp. T85-88), copied and prepared in advance. You could follow the game with a plenary discussion about problems which occur frequently in your teaching context and about possible solutions to the problems in the game.

Time out, take five

**Journal entry: Why bother with a
plan at all?** *(page 105)*   I 10 min

This journal entry encourages trainees to draw some final conclusions about lesson planning.

14 DON'T PANIC!
Classroom management

In this unit... trainees work on their classroom management skills. This unit also relates to Unit 15 *Us and them* about classroom interaction.

Reflection

TASK 1 Speak for yourself *(pages 106-107)* 20 min

The aim of this task is to discuss the use of English and L1 in class. It assumes that the teacher is teaching a monolingual class although parts of the task are relevant to teachers of multilingual classes.

Step 1

1 Elicit one or two examples to warm trainees up.

2 and 3 Hold a plenary to draw some conclusions from the discussion.

Step 2

The aim of this step is to think of practical ways of encouraging learners to speak English.

1 Some variables which influence how much English you speak in class:

- size of class
- learner motivation
- level of learners' English
- how much you need to control a class (secondary school pupils are probably better disciplined in L1)
- the learners' own language (in multilingual classes you need to speak English)
- how much other teachers in an institution speak English
- school or department policy
- knowledge of English
- how much English learners are used to hearing in class.

2 Some ways to encourage learners to speak English:

- Discuss your reasons for speaking English to learners (you can do this in L1 or in English). Some possible arguments for this are: it is a chance to practise English; doing communicative activities enables them to speak more, for example in groups.
- Ask learners to translate your instructions for others in the class, to avoid speaking L1 yourself.
- Speak English yourself as much as possible.
- Do warming-up activities in English.
- Use gesture and visuals.
- Place yourself near the group(s) you think will speak the least English at the beginning of an activity.
- Move around the class so that groups are at least obliged to speak English if you are near.
- Give your activity a time limit.
- Give someone in each group the task of reminding the group members to speak English.
- Remind learners before they do an activity to speak English and keep reminding them.
- Use very controlled activities at first, to get learners used to speaking to each other in English and gradually move into less controlled activities.

Observation

TASK 2 On the move *(pages 107-109)* 40 min

Note that this task and **Task 3 Silent movie** could be interpreted differently in different cultures where body language and eye contact can mean different things. Use these tasks as you see fit for training in different cultures.

The aim of this observation task is to look at a teacher's teaching space, body language and eye contact. This task can help trainees to see the value of using their bodies effectively in the classroom.

Step 1

The trainees observe a lesson in three stages:

1 For the first ten minutes they observe a teacher's teaching space.

2 For the second ten minutes they observe a teacher's eye contact.

3 For the rest of the lesson, trainees observe a teacher's body language.

Show trainees the examples of completed observation sheets on page 108 and clarify the tasks before they observe.

Step 2

You can highlight the following in class after you have read or discussed trainees' responses to the questions.

1 Teaching space

- Teachers who move around a lot in their classrooms probably seem more dynamic.
- Some teachers maintain discipline from behind a desk, others by walking around the classroom.
- You can hold a class's attention if you move around a lot.

2 Eye contact

c Some overall effects of eye contact include:

- Looking your learners in the eye can give you good control.
- Not catching a learner's eyes might indicate unconsciously to her that you are intimidated by her or that you are ignoring her.
- Catching a learner's eye and holding it when, for example, she is speaking out of turn can bring a learner's attention back to the class.
- Catching the eyes of other learners very briefly while one is speaking can keep the attention of a class.
- Avoiding eye contact with an over-talkative learner can stop her from talking too much.
- Avoiding eye contact while monitoring group work (looking at the table, the floor, etc.) helps a group to keep working while you are standing nearby.

3 Body language

2 Some reasons for using clear body language:

- to add actions to your voice
- to convey the meaning of something
- to manage a class
- to liven up a story or explanation.

Managing

TASK 3 Silent movie *(page 109)*   30-40 min

This game practises body language for classroom management. Note that there are some gestures which are acceptable in some cultures and not in others, so avoid any culturally unacceptable gestures during this activity.

The game is played in groups of four to eight. The rules of the game are on page 109. Photocopy and cut up enough sets of the **Silent movie cards** (p. T89) for each group. Explain the rules and do some examples before beginning.

Microteaching

TASK 4 In the hot seat

(page 110)  40-50 min

In this microteaching lesson, trainees practise using some of the classroom management skills studied in this unit. Ask a number of trainees (perhaps 4 or 6) to choose and prepare in advance one of the activities to last for about five minutes; ask each trainee to prepare a different one. When they teach, they should indicate which activity they have chosen and then receive feedback on that particular aspect of classroom management.

Time out, take five

Journal entry: Challenges in classroom management *(page 110)*   10 min

Here trainees reflect on their own greatest challenges in classroom management and possible work that they can do to improve them.

15 US AND THEM
Learning styles and classroom interaction

In this unit... trainees learn about learning styles and think about how to accommodate them in teaching English; they also learn about group dynamics and interacting with learners. This unit also relates to Unit 14 Don't panic! on classroom management.

Learning styles
Reflection

TASK 1 Curtain up *(pages 111-112)* 40 min

This task aims to guide trainees to find out their own perceptual learning style and to begin thinking about the implications for teaching. There are many different categorisations of learning styles; this is an easy-to-understand test, both for teachers and learners, based on work done by Reid and Kinsella (see Reid 1995); it reveals whether you are primarily a visual, auditory or kinaesthetic learner.

Step 1

Use question 1 as a warming-up activity.

Ensure that trainees understand the scoring method in the questionnaire. Each trainee will need a copy of the **Questionnaire: Learning styles** on page T90. Ask them if they agree with the results of the questionnaire.

Step 2

Key:

Responses to questions 1 to 4 are individual.

5 For example, if you are listening to a lecture and you are a weak auditory learner, you can write notes or make diagrams (thus drawing on visual and/or kinaesthetic learning styles).

6 It is quite likely that a teacher teaches in a way that benefits learners with the same learning styles as hers.

TASK 2 Acting out *(page 112)*   40-45 min

The aim of this task is to think about ways of accommodating auditory, visual and kinaesthetic learners in your lessons. You need to have done **Task 1 Curtain up** in order to do this task.

Step 1

Some more suggestions are:

VISUAL LEARNERS

- Ask a teacher to write instructions down for you.
- Write things down on index cards to help you remember things.
- Rewrite your notes when you are revising.
- Study in a quiet place.
- Use coloured pens to help you highlight your notes or to take notes.
- File notes under colours.
- If someone gives you oral instructions only, write them down for later.
- Try to recall a class or your notes on the page visually.
- Make drawings or diagrams of what you are learning.

AUDITORY LEARNERS

- If you don't understand, ask the teacher to repeat something.
- Involve yourself in group discussions.
- Tell someone else about what you are learning.
- Solve problems out loud before writing down your solution.
- If you don't understand diagrams, etc., get someone to explain to you orally.
- Tape classes and listen to them at home.
- Read aloud.
- If studying from a book, tell yourself out aloud what you imagine will come up in a chapter, or summarise out loud what you have read.
- Act out what you are learning.

KINAESTHETIC LEARNERS

- If you can't sit still in class, move a part of your body that won't disturb others.
- Study lying down – on your back or on your stomach, or in a variety of places.
- Use colour when you study, e.g. use coloured paper, study somewhere where you like the colours of the surroundings.
- Write notes while studying, e.g. make lists, diagrams.
- Use information transfer, i.e. make a diagram out of a written paragraph or try to draw what you are learning.
- Stretch between study periods.
- Involve yourself in activities in class.
- Think about what you are studying while you do sport.
- Doodle as you study.

Step 2

In this step, trainees think about ways of introducing vocabulary to accommodate auditory, visual and kinaesthetic learners. Collect together their ideas at the end of the task.

Classroom interaction
Reflection

TASK 3 Many hands make light work
(pages 113-114)   20-30 min

The aim of this task is for trainees to reflect on groups they have belonged to and decide what makes a group effective.

Step 1

Hold a brief plenary to hear some anecdotes from trainees about successful and unsuccessful groups that they have experienced.

Step 2

Question **3**:

Successful groups[1]

- are cohesive
- have a supportive, positive atmosphere; communication is open

---

[1] Many of these are based on Hadfield (1992: 11-12) and Stanford (1990).

- group members can compromise and decide on things together
- group members listen to each other and are interested in each other
- the group cooperates; members trust, accept and understand each other
- there is a sense of fun
- members are responsible for each other and the group
- problems are confronted openly and conflicts resolved constructively.

Unsuccessful groups
- have little cohesion
- have a tense or uncomfortable or over-quiet atmosphere
- individuals focus only on their own goals
- members don't listen to each other; members aren't interested in each other
- there is little trust, cooperation, or group responsibility; members aren't self-confident
- the atmosphere in the group is not one of fun
- some members don't participate, others dominate
- the group experiences conflicts (both with teacher and with each other).

Step 3

Hold a plenary to hear some of the trainees' ideas.

Observation

TASK 4 Criss-cross
(pages 114-115) 45 min (excluding observation)

The aim of this observation task is to reflect on classroom interaction patterns.

Step 1

An example of a partially completed observation sheet can be found on page 114. Clarify the observation task before trainees do it.

Step 2

Key:

Answers to question 1 will be personal; sample answer to question 2:

- Interact with all of the class and do not concentrate on particular learners or only one area of the classroom. Reason: if some learners feel ignored, they might not participate.
- Interact randomly, dotting your attention around the class. Reason: if you go around the class predictably, learners will not concentrate until it is their turn.

- Try to maintain a good relationship with the class, by interacting fairly with them. Reason: if you treat learners as fairly as possible, they will trust you more and perhaps cooperate more with you.

Interaction

TASK 5 It takes all sorts *(pages 115-116)* 40-60 min

The main aim of this task is to discuss the problem of mixed ability classes and how to teach them.

Step 1

Major problems that Chitra, the teacher, faces:

- large classes
- no other English teachers in the school
- many teaching hours
- mixed ability classes.

Step 2

Some further advice for Chitra:

- Allow a free period (e.g. 20-30 min per week), in which learners are allowed to choose own task/ material (e.g. book to read). A library of materials could benefit a large class with mixed ability.
- Sometimes make mixed ability groups; give higher level learners a specific task where they have to help the lower level learners.
- Practise writing in groups so you have less marking.
- Get a spokesperson from each group to report to the teacher in class the results of the group work.

TASK 6 Problem-solving *(pages 116-117)* 30-40 min

The aim of this task is for trainees to practise solving problems that they might come across while teaching.

Step 1

You can ask the groups to study all the case studies and find solutions or, alternatively, ask different groups to work on separate case studies.

Alternative: trainees read the case studies for homework and do the role-playing (Step 2) in class.

Step 2

Trainees role-play their solutions.

Possible actions:

Case study one: Grammar
Study the difference yourself between the present perfect and past tenses; apologise to the class for the mixed-up explanation and for getting angry with

46 ► TRAINER'S NOTES

them. Explain the difference clearly between the two tenses again, using a different presentation method.

Case study two: Georgi
Arrange to meet Georgi outside class. Explain that you want him to treat you as a teacher when he is in class.

Case study three: Kara
Have a serious talk to Kara after class one day, stating that you want her to cooperate. Explain to her your reasons for getting people to work with different partners sometimes (you can learn different things from different people, you can get to know other learners). Ask her for her opinion, too.

Case study four: Freddy
See Freddy after class and give him some extra homework. Make sure the rest of the class know about it, so that they will continue to do their homework. Next time, give someone who hasn't done their homework extra work on the spot.

A follow-on or alternative to this activity is for trainees or you to create case studies which are relevant to your own situation and to discuss and role-play them.

TASK 7 Virtual reality *(pages 117-118)*   25-35 min

The aim of this task is for trainees to experience a simulation and to reflect on how well they can listen and handle difficult situations, particularly in relation to teaching. Trainees change roles three times and experience three conflicts from different points-of-view. Copy and cut out the role cards (pp. T91-92) in advance.

Steps 1, 2 and 3   **G**

Trainees need to work in groups of three for the simulation to work effectively; if you do not have a number divisible by three, make one or two groups of four and ask one different member of the groups of four to sit out each time. Make sure the pace of the simulation is quick; each step does not need more than about five minutes for trainees to be able to get a flavour of the situation they are experiencing.

Step 4   **C**

Allow trainees first to express their initial impressions of the simulation, and then move on to the Focus questions.

Microteaching

TASK 8 Actions and reactions[2]
(page 118)   **G** and **M** 40-50 min

For this activity, trainees experience microteaching in large groups of eight to ten. Select trainees who you think can cope with classroom problems to do this microteaching task.

Teacher Role: the microteaching trainees or 'teachers' need to prepare for this activity in advance. Copy and give them their instructions for their Teacher Role on page 118 beforehand and explain to them that their 'learners' will be role-playing during the microteaching.

Trainees' roles: give each trainee one of the role cards on page T93, which they keep to themselves until the feedback stage.

Time out, take five

Journal entry: Me in a group
(page 119)   **I** 10 min

In this task, trainees reflect on their own role in a group and consolidate what they have learnt in the unit.

16 YOU CAN'T ALWAYS GET WHAT YOU WANT
Materials evaluation and adaptation

In this unit... trainees explore several aspects of materials evaluation and adaptation.

Materials evaluation

TASK 1 Straight from the horse's mouth
(page 120)   40 min

The aim of this task is to help trainees gain an awareness of how teachers select coursebooks.

Step 1   **P**

Prepare trainees for this task by helping them to find two English teachers to interview – someone else in their training institute, or teachers at a local secondary school, for example. You will need to provide them with copies of the **Interview: Coursebook analysis** (p. T94).

[2] This activity is based on one described in an article by Gołebiowska (1989).

16 YOU CAN'T ALWAYS GET WHAT YOU WANT 47

Step 2   **P** and **C**

In class trainees discuss the results of the questionnaire. Some suggested questions for a follow-up plenary discussion are:

- Were there any books commonly used and respected? If so, what aspect(s) did the teachers like about these books?
- What did the learners like or dislike about these books?
- Were there any books that were universally disliked?
- If so, why did the teachers feel they must continue to use these books?
- What was the single most important factor in selecting a coursebook?

Alternatives:

a Invite some teachers into your classroom for trainees to interview in class about the books they use.

b Invite trainees to interview you about your selecting this book or another book for another course.

TASK 2 At first glance *(pages 120-122)*   35-40 min

The aim of this task is to use one quick way to evaluate an English language coursebook.

Each pair of trainees needs to bring in a copy of a coursebook commonly used in their teaching situation that they would like to evaluate.

Step 1   **I**

Check to see that the trainees all understand the meaning of each of the nine components of *The MATERIALS Test* (p. 121).

Step 2   **P**

Each trainee needs a copy of the **Coursebook evaluation chart** (p. T95). Monitor trainees as they discuss *The MATERIALS Test*, complete the **Coursebook evaluation chart** and discuss question 3.

Step 3   **G**

Trainees form groups and present their case for adopting the coursebook, or not.

Time out, take five

Journal entry: Evaluating this book
(page 122)   **I** 10 min

Encourage trainees to send the authors of this book a copy of their journal entry. Your own feedback on the book would be equally welcome. For the authors' address, see page vii.

Materials adaptation

TASK 3 You can't always get what you want
(page 122)   10 min

The aim of this short task is to introduce four ways of adapting materials: change, remove, replace and add.

Step 1   **G**

Trainees brainstorm the ways they might adapt a coursebook. Accept all answers.

Step 2   **P**

Answers will vary.

TASK 4 Upon closer inspection
(pages 123-127)   40-60 min

This task prepares trainees for adapting materials themselves. Trainees each need a copy of the **Table: Inspecting activities** (p. T96).

Step 1   **P** and **G**

2 *Key:*

MOSAIC I	
I Skills work	
a listening	1a, 1b, 2, 4, 5a, 9
b speaking	1b, 3a, 5b, 9
c reading	3b
d writing	4, 10
e grammar	2, 5, 6
f pronunciation	1a, 2a, 5a, 7
g vocabulary	7, 10
II Real communicative interaction	3b and 5b aim toward real, two-way communication but stop short of it
III Learner interest: likely to motivate Ls	9 – game – likely to be fun
IV Aims of the unit (from the teacher's manual)	present and practise *to be* with *she/he*; present and practise countries and nationalities

Step 2   **G**

Trainees discuss the four sample adaptations.

TRAINER'S NOTES

Step 3

Collect the trainees' adaptations or copy and circulate them.

TASK 5 Learners do it themselves
(pages 127-128)   35-40 min

This task introduces trainees to three learner-based activities. Begin by asking the whole class what a 'learner-based activity' is and jot their answers on the board (see Glossary, p. viii-x).

Step 1   **G**

Some possible answers are listed below; accept or add any others that seem reasonable:

Learner-based materials

What materials can learners bring to class?

- photos, drawings or other visual materials
- music or other audio material
- information about themselves
- articles they find interesting
- excerpts from books they have read.

How can learner-based materials be used?

- Learners create their own stories, exercises or other activities for use by other learners in class.
- Learners listen to songs to catch lyrics and discuss possible interpretations.
- Learners write questions for each other.
- Teacher builds stories and activities around visuals learners bring in.

Step 2

Trainees discuss the advantages and disadvantages of using learner-based activities, then read the passage (p. 127) individually to confirm or revise their ideas.

1 Possible advantages are:

- Learners may be more motivated to participate.
- Learners may remember vocabulary, grammar, etc. more clearly or for a longer time if tasks are personally relevant.
- Learners may feel a greater sense of ownership of their English class, increasing their sense of personal responsibility for their own learning.
- Teacher may find work load reduced when learners actively contribute materials and tasks.

2 Possible disadvantages are:

- Teacher may lose some control of the class.
- Learners may not be prepared to participate or may not expect to be so active and responsible.
- Some learners may not contribute the materials or information.
- Class becomes less predictable for the teacher and learners, which could be potentially threatening to either party.

Step 3

Some possible answers are listed, though accept any others that seem reasonable.

1 Answers will vary. Ask them to support their general opinions with specific examples.

2 How a teacher can prepare learners for learner-based activities:

- A teacher can explain (perhaps in L1) why this type of activity can be useful: e.g. it may make the lesson more interesting for everyone, and everyone will get to know each other better.
- A teacher might suggest that they should first give the activity a try before deciding they won't like it.
- A teacher might explain that, in this type of task, learners have to take more responsibility: if they don't participate, the lesson will not be much fun for their classmates. The more effort they put into the activity, the more they will learn.

3 Answers will vary with the trainees and the teaching context.

a Potential difficulties:
- Learners may be confused at the beginning or perhaps too passive.
- It takes practice to get learners used to their new role.

b Overcoming difficulties:
- By starting with something that is short and likely to succeed, a teacher can hope to boost the confidence and motivation of the learners to continue doing learner-based lessons in the future.

Photocopy masters

49

Unit 2, Task 4 Shifting viewpoints

Role cards

GROUP 1

Role 1: Enthusiastic teacher

Imagine that this lesson is part of one you taught and is one that went very well. Take notes on all the positive aspects of your behaviour and the learners' actions to support your view of the lesson as a success.

GROUP 2

Role 2: Critical teacher

Imagine that this lesson is part of one you taught and is one that you felt did not go so well. Take notes on all the negative aspects of your own behaviour and the learners' actions to support your view of the lesson as more a failure than a success.

GROUP 3

Role 3: Supportive evaluator

Examine this portion of the lesson as a supportive evaluator, one who is inclined to focus on the positive and be optimistic. List as many positive features of the lesson as possible in the learners' actions and the teacher's actions.

GROUP 4

Role 4: Negative evaluator

Examine the lesson from the point of view of an evaluator who tends to make rather harsh criticisms and be pessimistic. Pay attention to those actions by the teacher which you consider to be mistakes or unhealthy. List as many negative remarks as you can.

Unit 2, Task 4 Shifting viewpoints

Lesson transcript

Students: Young adults (19-25 years old), upper intermediate
Class size: 17 (3 male, 14 female)
Furniture: Ls sit in chairs behind desks, scattered around the class, in pairs or threes, facing white board
Institution: Teacher training college

T: *[sits on table at front]* Is anybody else coming, or is this...? 1

[Several Ls name a learner who is missing.]

Today we're going to have discussions, in I think two or three small groups. This discussion is going to be about one of the 5 topics which is on the list here *[T shows worksheets he is holding]* and the first activity we're going to do today is... I'm going to give you this piece of paper and in pairs 10 I would like you to make notes for each statement. I'll hand it out and discuss it with you.

[T hands out worksheets, one to each L; on the worksheets is a list of controversial statements. 15 The late L arrives; learners laugh at her jokes as she enters the class.]

Erm. This is for forming opinions. You have to read carefully through the instructions; you have to make marks. If... you're reading 20 the statements... you say *I strongly agree*, you put two crosses; if you agree but not very strongly, put one; if you have no opinion, put a circle, and two minuses and one minus if you disagree or strongly 25 disagree.

[Students discuss statements in pairs; some confusion about what signs they should put next to each statement; Ls explain in L1 to each other. T goes around class and listens as Ls 30 discuss statements; he also makes quick lists of learners in preparation for dividing the class into smaller groups. Some laughter. About 10 minutes pass while pairs of Ls discuss statements. T returns to sit on table at front.] 35

I'm going to divide you up into three groups, so listen for your group. Group 1 is ...

[T reads out three lists of names which he prepared while the Ls were discussing the 40 statements. One name appears on two lists.]

Who am I missing? Well, we'll find out. Am I missing somebody? What I want you to do in the smaller group is to decide on one of these topics to talk about, or possibly two, 45 and choose one which you have differences about so that you can actually talk about it. Then find arguments for or against the statements and then later on you have to do the discussion in the group. So first decide 50 which topic you are going to talk about and then carry it out. OK? So let's have group 1 over here *[points to right of classroom]*, group 2 here *[points to back of room]* and group 3 there *[points to left of room]*. 55

[Ls move to their group's position, calling out the names of the people in their group or the number of their group. Some laughter. Ls start to discuss which statements to talk about.]

Unit 2, Task 6 Telescopic or microscopic viewing?

CLASS OBSERVATION TABLE A

Class .... *No. of learners* ....

Age of learners .... *Length of lesson* .... *Level* ....

Observer .... *Teacher observed* ....

USE THIS SIDE TO ANSWER QUESTIONS 1-7.

1. List all materials and equipment used in this lesson (e.g. textbook, blackboard, audio-visual aids).

2. What do you think the aim of the lesson was? Do you think the teacher's objectives were achieved? Give reasons.

3. How much time did the teacher talk compared to the amount of time learners spoke (e.g. 50-50%)?

4. How much time did the teacher use English compared to her native language (e.g. 20-80%)? How much time did the learners use English versus their native language?

5. Describe the learners' participation (very active for most of the time, etc.). How were the learners called upon? Did any volunteer?

6. What was the general behaviour and attitude of the learners during the lesson? What was the general atmosphere of the class?

7. How often did the teacher praise her learners? How were errors handled?

USE THE REVERSE SIDE TO ANSWER QUESTIONS 8-9

8. Use part of the reverse side to draw a sketch of the classroom. Notice what is on the walls and where any equipment is located. How are the desks arranged (in rows facing the blackboard, etc.)? Where is the teacher most of the time?

9. Use the rest of the back of this sheet to make notes on the different language activities in the order that they occurred (e.g. review of homework, 5 minutes, individual learners read aloud answers, teacher corrected errors).

Unit 2, Task 6 Telescopic or microscopic viewing?

Class observation table B
Use of transitions

Class _____   No. of learners _____   Age of learners _____   Length of lesson _____

Level _____   Observer _____   Teacher observed _____

Aims of the lesson _____

Materials used _____

Aims of the Observation Task

- To observe how a teacher makes transitions between one point in the lesson and the next task or activity which is different

- To reflect on how a teacher's marking transitions affects learners' ability to follow the lesson and see connections between the parts of the lesson

Instructions

When a teacher moves from one task or activity to the next, she often marks this point with a word, such as *OK*, *Now*, or a phrase or sentence, as in *I am going to ask you some questions*, or *And for my next point*. In your observation, examine a 45-50 minute lesson and look for the following points. As you observe, put a tick (✔) in the appropriate boxes in the left-hand column. If you have time, write down in the right-hand column the word(s) used for the transitions. One example is provided.

Transitions markers	Actual words used by the teacher
a word	
a phrase/sentence ✔	*Now let's do some reading, OK?*
pause/silence	
other (write here):	

Add up the results: For each of the above categories, what was the total? Write this number in each box and circle it. How many transitions were there in the entire lesson?

TOTAL NUMBER: _____

Post-observation questions

1 Which kind of transition did the teacher use most often?

2 Did the teacher use one transition marker several times?

3 Which transitions seemed the clearest to you?

4 Choose two of the transitions. Write an alternative transition for each one.

5 What have you learnt from doing this observation task?

Unit 3, Task 5 Jumbled grammar

Jumbled lesson plan

a Hold up photo of girl asking boy a question. Tell class she's asking him *Would you like to go to the cinema?* and write q on board.

b Ls listen to tape to confirm their answers to matching task. Ls check answers in pairs.

c Practise question and answers using *Would you like to...?* with individual Ls and L–L.

d Ask Ls what they think the boy might reply to question and write up some of their ideas. Try to elicit responses in book p.88 ('*Yes, I'd love to*'; '*Sorry, I...*')

e Check Ls understand and/or explain that *would* is used as an invitation here.

f In closed pairs, Ls try to find out what their partner would like to do at the weekend, using the question *Would you like to...?*

g Ls look at listening task (p.88) and try to match questions with answers in their book before they listen - guessing the answers. (e.g. of question and answer in book '*Would you like to come swimming?*' '*Sorry, I'm going to the disco.*')

h Ls listen to four conversations on tape and follow the language in the box on p.88.

i Ls look at the box on p.88. (Box contains questions and answers with *Would you like to...?* e.g. '*Would you like to come to a party tomorrow?*' '*Yes, I'd love to.*')

j Ls write down for themselves four activities they would like to do at the weekend. Elicit example. Write on board: e.g. *I would like to see a film.*

k Play tape of four conversations, this time version with gaps in; Ls listen and fill in the gaps.

l Elicit and check answers to gap-filling listening task.

m Aims of lesson: listening for specific information; introducing and practising *Would you like to...?*; making and responding to invitations.

n Materials needed: tape recorder, photo of girl talking to a boy, textbook, teacher's book, tape.

54

Unit 3, Task 6 Drawing it out

Observation table: eliciting

Class _____   Number of learners _____   Age of learners _____   Length of lesson _____

Level _____   Observer _____   Teacher observed _____

Aims of the lesson _____

_____

_____

Materials used _____

1 What is elicited	2 What teacher says when eliciting	3 Learner's response (exact words)	4 Teacher's reaction to learner	5 Body language/ visuals used
By bus.	*Jules, how do you come to school?*	*On bus.*	*Not quite. On bus? What do we say in English?*	*T repeats sentence, looking doubtful as she repeats.*

Unit 3, Task 7 The eliciting game

Eliciting cards

six *how* questions in the present tense	four examples of comparatives of adjectives ending in *-y* (e.g. *lovely* → *lovelier*)	1st and 3rd persons of the verb *have got*	six past tense questions with *where* and *did* (e.g. *Where did you see it?*)
five examples of past tense questions with irregular verbs	six examples of sentences with *like + -ing*	five questions with *have got* in the 1st and 3rd person	three examples of the present continuous tense in the 1st person and three examples in the 3rd person
five examples of past tense statements with irregular verbs	six examples of sentences with *hate + gerund (-ing* verb form)	five examples of *there is* and *there are*	the past continuous tense 1st, 2nd and 3rd persons
the use of the present continuous tense	three examples of *if...will* sentences	three sentences using *much* and three using *many*	six examples of the present continuous tense used as the future
the use of the present simple tense	the word order of sentences in the present perfect with *just*	past tense of the verb *to be* (all persons)	the negative form of *have got* for all persons
six examples of the use of the simple present tense	the prepositions: *on, over, above, below, beneath*	three questions using *Is there any?* and *Are there any?*	the negative of the past tense: examples for all persons
the use of the present perfect tense using *just*	the past tense of the modal verb *can* (= *could*)	six questions using *whose?*	*too* and *enough* with adjectives: three examples of each
past participles of the verbs: *eat, sleep, get up, go to bed*	six sentences illustrating the difference between *for, since* and *ago*	the possessive pronouns *my, your, his, her*	*can* and *can't*: all persons
past tense of the verbs: *eat, sleep, get up, go to bed*	six examples of sentences with *he/she can*	questions with *be* (all persons)	six examples of sentences using *let's*
four examples of comparatives of adjectives with three or more syllables (e.g. *interesting* → *more interesting*)	five examples of sentences using the past continuous tense with *I* and *when* (e.g. *I was -ing when...*)	six past tense questions with *what* and *did* (e.g. *What did you do?*)	present perfect tense with *since* and *for*: three examples of each

Unit 5, Task 2 Do as I say

Observation table: Instruction-giving skills

Class _____   Number of learners _____   Age of learners _____   Length of lesson _____

Level _____   Observer _____   Teacher observed _____

Aims of the lesson _____

_____

_____

Materials used _____

Instruction-giving skills	Circle appropriate number	Comments
signalling of beginning of activity	clear 4—3—2—① unclear	*T did not tell Ls when activity began*
stating of aims	clear 4—3—2—1 unclear	
voice	clear 4—3—2—1 unclear	
eliciting information from learners	clear 4—3—2—1 unclear	
use of examples	clear 4—3—2—1 unclear	
eye movement to hold attention	clear 4—3—2—1 unclear	
mime, gesture or other body language	clear 4—3—2—1 unclear	
repeating instructions in a different way	clear 4—3—2—1 unclear	
asking questions to check understanding	clear 4—3—2—1 unclear	
use of simple language	clear 4—3—2—1 unclear	
management and organisation of the class	clear 4—3—2—1 unclear	
use of visual aids (e.g. board, role cards, worksheets, pictures, real objects)	clear 4—3—2—1 unclear	
signalling of end of activity	clear 4—3—2—1 unclear	
other (write here)	clear 4—3—2—1 unclear	
other	clear 4—3—2—1 unclear	

Unit 5, Task 5 Paving the way

Pre-writing activities

Pre-writing activity A: Using a picture

You want to arouse your class's interest in the writing topic, by using this photograph.

Create some questions for your class using the photo. For example, *What time is it? Where has Jerry been?*

Pre-writing activity B: Listening

You want your class to listen to the conversation that the parents are having just before the teenager arrives home. Invent a dialogue you think they might have, and record it on to a cassette or write it down to read out later. Then decide exactly how you will use the conversation as a pre-writing activity, by creating an activity for your class. Begin like this:

Father: I'm going to call the police.
Mother: No, not yet. Let's just wait a few minutes longer.

Pre-writing activity C: Brainstorming

You want the class to think about some possible topics in the conversation between the teenager and his parents, in other words to brainstorm as many ideas as possible.

Design some questions which will help the class to think about the topics of the conversation between the family members. For example, *When you come home late, what questions do your parents ask you?* or *How do parents react when a teenager comes home late?*

Pre-writing activity D: Clustering

You want your class to brainstorm possible vocabulary that will be used in the conversation, using a technique called *clustering* or *mind mapping*. Here is an example of a mind map, using the word

holidays

Think of a key word (or phrase) which you hope will produce vocabulary linked to your writing topic and which learners can use in their dialogue. Write the word up in the middle of the board and ask the class to shout out associated words or phrases. Accept any responses and put them on the mind map, grouping associated words together, until the board or page is covered with words.

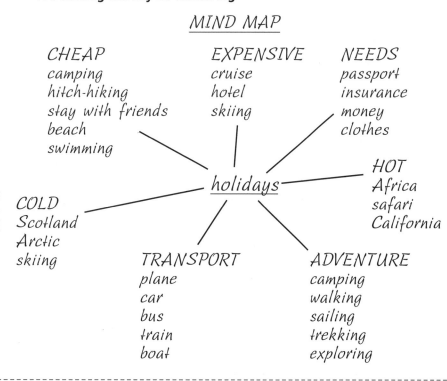

Unit 6, Task 3 Eavesdropping on a teacher

Observation table: Teaching listening

Class _____ Number of learners _____ Age of learners _____ Length of lesson _____

Level _____ Observer _____ Teacher observed _____

Aims of the lesson _____

_____

_____

Materials used _____

Kind of preparation	Time spent on preparation	Purpose stated (Yes/No)	Type of passage, topic and length (min)	No. of times passage heard
T showed picture of father and daughter and elicited what they might be talking about. T gave true/false questions out before tape was started.	*5 minutes*	*No*	*Dialogue between father and daughter (3 minutes)*	*2*

Unit 6, Task 4 And the winner is...

Teaching listening techniques

Teaching listening techniques	Score	Advantage(s)	Disadvantage(s)
a Teacher plays a tape, without introducing the topic or anything else.	4	*None*	*No preparation for listening; no purpose stated*
b Teacher tells learners their purpose in listening.			
c The teacher announces the topic of the passage then asks class to brainstorm vocabulary they expect to hear in the passage.			
d Teacher asks learners to predict questions that might be asked in a taped conversation.			
e Teacher plays the taped passage once, without preparation, asking the learners to listen for the main ideas.			
f Learners have done one listening task to get the main idea of a text. For the second time they listen, the teacher gives a task to listen for more detailed information.			
g Teacher asks learners to listen to the tape and then summarise the content in their own language.			
h Teacher asks learners to draw something (e.g. a picture or map) while listening.			
i Teacher plays each sentence of a taped dialogue and asks learners to translate the sentence into their L1.			
j Teacher dictates a passage to learners, leaving gaps between phrases; learners write down exactly what they hear.			
k Teacher plays a short passage, then orally asks learners basic comprehension questions.			
l Teacher plays the same passage a few times, each time asking learners to do a new listening activity and listen for a different purpose.			
m Teacher gives the class the text to read as they listen to the tape.			

Unit 7, Task 3 Talking the hind leg off a donkey

Talking the hind leg off a donkey

	Activity A Drawing a picture	Activity B Role-play	Activity C Parent power
a What language (e.g. grammar, vocabulary, functions) does the activity aim to produce?		*Questions mostly in present tense; everyday (home) vocab.*	
b How effectively will the activity generate the language that it aims to produce?			
c What preparation will the class need to do it?			
d How much will everyone participate in the activity?	*Describer will probably say more.*		
e Is there an information gap in the activity?			
f How much English will the learners speak?			*Equal amount — but not much (Yes, they do/ No, they don't)*
g How interesting and enjoyable is the activity for your own learners?	*Fun: nice for learners to draw picture.*		
h Do the learners have short or long speaking turns?			*Quite short.*
i What problems can you foresee with this activity?		*Learners only read the cards and don't play their roles.*	

Unit 7, Task 5 Chatterbox

Teacher's instructions

Your task is to teach a speaking activity, called Spot the Difference. Below are two similar pictures of a speaking class. Divide your class into pairs, A and B. Give learners A copies of picture A and learners B copies of picture B. They must NOT look at each other's pictures; if possible, sit A and B back to back. A and B must discover what the ten differences between their pictures are by asking and answering Yes/No questions.

To prepare

a Think through the instructions you will give (describe what they will do, explain about the pictures, divide them into pairs, sit them back to back, tell them when to begin).

b Try to think how you will get learners to speak English during the activity, and what you will say in English.

c Decide what you will do when they are doing the activity (walk around the class listening, take down mistakes, sit at the front of the class, join in).

d Decide how long the learners need for the activity and stop it at an appropriate moment.

e Decide what to do immediately after the activity: correct all the mistakes?; correct some mistakes?; praise the class?; round the activity off with a remark?

Differences between Picture A and Picture B

1 teacher with/without glasses
2 one class has two extra girl pupils in it
3 writing on blackboard different
4 pupil in A smiling/same pupil in B grumpy
5 several torn up papers under a desk in picture A, not in picture B
6 A: teacher with group at front of class; B: teacher with group at back of class
7 In the one group where the pupils are not working: pupils are chatting together in A; pupils are playing with something not to do with the lesson together in B.
8 B: on one table is pencil case; on same table in A no pencil case
9 A: sun is shining outside; B: clouds/rain outside
10 A kitten is climbing out of a pupil's bag in B: no kitten in A

Unit 7, Task 7 The atmosphere game

The atmosphere game

Rules

1 Roll both dice. The highest scorer begins.

2 The first player rolls one die (for the horizontal numbers). Then she rolls the second die (for the vertical numbers), e.g. If you roll a 3 with the horizontal die and a 2 with the vertical one, you put your counter on the square which says 'Divide a class into groups, with both words and gestures.'

3 Look at the situation on the square your counter is on and read it aloud to your group. Then say, in your own words, exactly what you would say to the class in the situation. Do not give a solution, but say precisely the words you would say to the class.

4 The rest of the group must give you feedback about what you say; if they are not completely satisfied, try again. Look at the following criteria when giving feedback:

- tact
- simplicity of English
- encouragement skills
- clarity
- body language/gesture
- improvisation skills

5 The next player now takes their turn. If a player lands on a square which has already been used, he throws again.

Die 1 → Die 2 ↓	1	2
1	Encourage a learner who keeps on speaking L1 to speak more English.	Role-play a conversation with your class about a sports match or a television programme which happened yesterday evening.
2	Two learners are angry because you have split them up; role-play a conversation with them after class, explaining your reasons to them.	Your class is rather over-excited and noisy; tell them tactfully to be quieter.
3	React tactfully to one learner who has said, *That's rubbish!* about another learner's contribution.	Explain to a group of learners why they should not laugh at others' mistakes.
4	Elicit information from the other players in your group about a topic they choose.	Set up an activity where learners must work in groups to decide on ten practical improvements for their school.
5	Encourage a learner to say something about their English lessons, by asking short questions.	Set up an activity where learners must ask each other in pairs about their weekend.
6	Encourage a shy learner to say more (other players decide on a topic for you).	Tactfully tell a learner who talks a lot to keep quiet for a while.

3	4	5	6
Get one learner to ask another learner some questions on the topic of music.	One learner has spoken very enthusiastically about her favourite singer; give some positive feedback.	Discourage two learners from laughing at others in the class; explain your reasons why you think it is unacceptable.	Find out some personal information about your learners' families, by asking simple questions.
Divide a class into groups, with both words and gestures.	Set up a pair work activity. First, tell them one of them will describe their bedroom and the other will draw it. Then, divide the class clearly into pairs, with both words and gestures.	Get your class to ask some facts about your family in simple English.	You have set up a group work activity where learners must ask and answer questions from a questionnaire. Check learners have understood the instructions for the activity: do not say, *Do you understand?* but ask simple questions to check.
Set up an activity where learners must work in groups. In the activity, the learners choose together which candidate out of four should win a prize for bravery.	Give some tactful positive feedback to a shy learner who is beginning to participate in speaking activities.	Explain to your class in simple English why you want them to speak English during speaking activities.	Apologise to a class in simple English about not having given clear instructions.
Give positive feedback to two learners who have voiced opposite opinions on the topic of animal rights.	Give instructions in two different ways for a speaking activity where learners role-play a scene in a shoe shop.	Make an encouraging remark after a class has completed a discussion on a recent event in the news.	You are collecting information together after a group work activity; role-play how you will do this.
A learner said, *I go bus yesterday*. Encourage him to self-correct (another player plays the learner).	Explain to two students who do not want to work together your reasons for wanting them to work together.	Disagree with a learner about their opinion but do not reject them personally (other players choose the topic).	You are rather irritated because your class spoke too much L1 during a speaking activity. Role-play a conversation with them about this (the other players play your learners.)
A learner is telling you about her pet; have a conversation with her, showing genuine interest in what she is saying.	Think of and say five different ways of saying 'well done' to a class.	Get your class to ask you in simple English about your weekend.	Give instructions for a speaking activity from this unit.

Unit 8, Task 1 Private eye

Observation table: Real-life reading

Class _____   Number of learners _____   Age of learners _____   Length of lesson _____

Level _____   Observer _____   Teacher observed _____

Aims of the lesson _____

_____

_____

Materials used _____

Who?	What? Text Type	Where?	How? Posture and Manner	Why?
young man	newspaper (someone else's)	on train	standing; stealthily peering over someone else's shoulder	to get information, because curious

Unit 8, Task 1 Private eye

Observation table: Classroom reading

Class _____   Number of learners _____   Age of learners _____   Length of lesson _____

Level _____   Observer _____   Teacher observed _____

Aims of the lesson _____

_____

_____

Materials used _____

Who?	**What?** Text Type	**How?** Posture and Manner	**Why?**	**Other** **comments**
two students	*coursebook dialogue*	*seated across the room from each other, reading aloud*	*to practise pronunciation*	*rest of class a bit bored? distracted?*

Unit 8, Task 2 The tortoise or the hare?

Which reading strategies are effective?

Reading strategies	Effective (E) or Ineffective (I)	Reasons
a use my finger to help my eyes follow lines of text		
b read each word very carefully in order to understand the entire text		
c keep my eyes moving past the unfamiliar words and thus try to understand the main ideas		
d say words quietly to myself		
e write the meaning of new words in L1 in margin of page		
f look up unfamiliar words in a bilingual dictionary		
g start reading without panicking or thinking *Help! I'm not going to understand*		
h look for linking words that help explain relationship between sentences (e.g. *in contrast, for example*)		
i ask my teacher for help whenever I meet an unfamiliar word		
j use different reading strategies to read different types of texts		
k translate a difficult section of text into L1		
l think of other words I already know that are similar to the unknown word(s) I come across		
m find the sentence that contains the main idea		
n read a lot of different things in order to expand my vocabulary and improve my general comprehension		
o study or write vocabulary lists and translations of words into L1		
p try to understand the relationship between the main ideas and supporting details		
q look at titles, subtitles, pictures and other visuals before reading	*E*	*Can help orient the reader*
r read a text very quickly the first time to get the gist (main idea)		
s underline or highlight words I don't understand		
t create some questions for myself before I read which I think or hope the text will answer		
u limit myself to looking up in the dictionary only a few unknown words		
v circle or highlight key words in a bright colour		

Unit 8, Task 5 Upside down, inside out

Jumbled lesson plan

a Reading activity: 'True or False?' Ls decide if statements about the main ideas in the text (*Fads and Trends in the USA*) are true or false.

b Pairs. Ls do exercise 'Guessing Vocabulary'. Ls guess the meaning of key vocabulary (*lifestyle, in fashion, out of date, influence, slang*) from context, looking at example sentences from passage. Check Ls understand.

c Groups. Discussion – elicit/suggest a recent trend (e.g. mobile telephones, computers, a recent fashion); in groups, Ls discuss advantages and disadvantages of the trend they choose.

d Assign homework: 'Building Vocabulary and Study Skills: Fads and Trends'.

e Give/ask for answers to 'True or False?' Clarify any problems.

f Collect answers to reading structure exercise.

g Pairs. Ls do exercise 'Understanding Reading Structure': identifying topic sentence of each paragraph from article.

h Look at pictures related to fads and trends in the US. Ls discuss pictures in pairs: predict topics article will mention.

i Introduce topic of new unit: fads and trends. Pre-teach or elicit *fad* and *trend*. Ls brainstorm examples from their own experience: collect on board.

j Collect ideas about Ls' predictions on board.

Unit 8, Task 7 If the shoe doesn't fit...

Situation cards (1)

Your class of 40 learners, aged 12-13, act restless and inattentive while two pupils read a dialogue from the textbook aloud. What can you do to resolve this situation?

You notice that one learner's textbook is completely covered with notes in L1, all direct translations of new vocabulary. You want to suggest an alternative reading strategy which he might try.

You ask your intermediate-level learners to paraphrase a short reading they have just read. One learner does not understand *paraphrase*. Find another way to explain the term and its purpose.

Your class has just read a short autobiography about Diego Maradona, the famous Argentinian football player. Suggest one possible post-reading activity for them.

You want your learners to practise making inferences about a text. Give an example or two of an *inference*, then explain (in English) what it means.

Your class is going to read an article entitled 'Fatal Accident on West Road'. Invent three questions to help them understand the text.

Several learners ask about the meaning of the word *influence*. Although they want you to translate it, you prefer to explain it in English. How would you do that?

You ask your class the following question about a text: *Do you think Mrs Saunders will believe the police?* No one understands you. What would you do next?

You want to motivate learners to read English more, using available resources in your area. Tell them three places they can find resources written in English.

Your class has just read a conversation between three learners about an end-of-term party. Suggest one possible post-reading activity for them.

Learners are working individually on comprehending a reading passage. You want them to work cooperatively instead. What might you do to build teamwork?

You want to make the classroom atmosphere where you are sitting now more relaxed and homelike to encourage learners to read English for pleasure during the last ten minutes of class. What could you do to change the ambience?

Your learners read an article, 'Quakes: Their Causes and Effects'. When you ask, *What are some examples of devastating effects of earthquakes?*, no one answers. Re-phrase the question in simpler English.

You want your high-beginning level learners to practise scanning. You hand them a copy of an English-language culture magazine, with listings of films, theatres, etc. What type of scanning task could you give them?

Unit 8, Task 7 If the shoe doesn't fit...

Situation cards (2)

Your aim is to help your beginning-level learners skim reading passages before they read them more carefully. Explain to them what *skimming* is and why it is a useful strategy.

Your class has just read the cover of a CD about a famous pop group. Invent an interview situation to follow on from this activity. Which roles would you ask your learners to play? What would the interview be about?

You want to check whether your low-advanced level learners understand the relationship between sentences in a chronologically organised passage. What technique would you use? How does this technique work?

Your class is going to read an article about three lions which savaged and nearly killed a man who jumped into their den at London Zoo. Invent three questions for them to answer as they read the article to help them understand what happened.

The newspaper article you are going to read with your class is accompanied by a photograph of a large crowd of people, looking angry. How could you use this photo to motivate them to read?

Your class has just read a text about young people drinking a lot of alcohol. Invent a role-play to follow on from the text.

Your class is going to read a passage entitled 'Mistaken Identity'; how might you use the title to interest them in the passage?

You are going to read an article with your class about camping holidays; invent five questions involving a personal response from your learners about the topic.

Explain to your class five reasons for reading in English.

Explain to your class in simple English two reasons for not underlining every word they do not know in a reading passage.

Give three arguments for reading aloud and three arguments against it.

Your class has just read an article about the causes and effects of air pollution. Suggest a follow-up activity which relates closely to this topic.

Unit 9, Task 1 To whom it may concern

Writing assignment A

You are going to write a short composition on the following topic: 'Why I Want to Be an English Teacher.'

1 Write a preliminary outline or some notes. Take about 10 minutes.

2 Write your composition. You have 20 minutes to write and check it for mistakes in grammar and mechanics (e.g. spelling and punctuation). Your trainer will read your finished composition.

Writing assignment B

A magazine for English language teachers has announced a contest! You are invited to submit a short article (maximum: three paragraphs in length), explaining why you want to be an English teacher. The winning entry will be published in an upcoming issue, and its author will receive a prize: one year's subscription to the magazine, plus a new comprehensive dictionary of American idioms and slang.

I PLANNING AHEAD

A Before you write, spend five minutes jotting down whatever comes into your head about the following:

Reasons I like teaching English   *My favourite things about learning English*

B Circle the two most interesting reasons you gave for why you like teaching English and write a sentence about each of them. Take five minutes.

1

2

II INTRODUCTION

Think about how you want to begin your composition. Again, take five minutes. Think about what will grab the attention of your readers, other English teachers. Something funny? Something mysterious? Example:

I have to confess: my motivation for teaching English is ... the money! In fact, ...

Write one *possible* introductory sentence here:

III WRITING

Spend 15 minutes writing three paragraphs: an introduction, a paragraph explaining your most important reason and a concluding paragraph, as follows:

- Begin with your power-packed introductory sentence.
- Look back at I B: PLANNING AHEAD. Decide which your most favourite thing about teaching English is and write one paragraph about that idea. Be sure to give enough details to support your idea.
- Finish with a concluding paragraph. Example: *All things considered, I like helping people grow, and teaching is an immensely satisfying way for me to accomplish that.*

GOOD LUCK!

Unit 9, Task 6 Writer's block (1)

Problem cards

1 Writer's block: a learner feels terror when faced with a blank page; he cannot write anything.

9 A learner fails to include a conclusion in his essay.

17 A learner writes a long paragraph in very long sentences, using too many words.

25 A group of learners doesn't want to write together on a group writing project.

2 A learner has trouble writing enough: his writing is too brief.

10 A learner has no knowledge about his topic.

18 The writer does not achieve his aim, to persuade his reader of something.

26 After finishing writing, a learner wants to continue to focus on the topic of whales, but is tired of writing.

3 A learner is bored with the topic of his writing assignment.

11 A learner needs more time than all the other learners to complete a writing activity.

19 The class says they would like to get a real response to their writing from somebody else beside their teacher.

WILD CARD
Invent a problem that is common in your teaching context.

4 A learner has trouble with the traditional assignments (all compositions) given in the textbook.

12 A learner believes that writing in English is only used in school instead of in 'real life'.

20 A learner copies his friend's paragraph and turns it in as his own writing.

WILD CARD
Invent a problem that is common in your teaching context.

5 A learner finds it hard to write by himself.

13 A learner was supposed to write an article for a teenage magazine, but writes an essay-type article for the teacher.

21 A learner has insufficient notes to write an essay.

WILD CARD
Invent a problem that is common in your teaching context.

6 A learner has written a lot but his writing has too little information.

14 A learner uses the same basic words over and over again, boring the reader.

22 A learner has no knowledge of a particular text type (e.g. business letter).

WILD CARD
Invent a problem that is common in your teaching context.

7 A learner writes only in generalisations and includes few supporting details.

15 The class is unmotivated to write assignments given by the teacher.

23 A learner writes without punctuation *or* in long sentences with only commas as punctuation.

WILD CARD
Invent a problem that is common in your teaching context.

8 A learner omits an introduction to his paragraph.

16 The story a learner hands in shifts confusingly back and forth between the narrator's viewpoint and the main character's viewpoint.

24 A learner writes one long paragraph filled with many different ideas.

WILD CARD
Invent a problem that is common in your teaching context.

Unit 9, Task 6 Writer's block (2)

Solution cards

a Show the learner a model text of the type he is to write.

i Expand the writer's vocabulary by reading and doing vocabulary development exercises; learn synonyms for several words.

q Practise shortening the writing: find key words and ideas. Re-write the paragraph, shortening it by a sentence each time.

y Suggest post-writing activities on same topic: e.g. find article(s) for learner to read, organise role-plays between journalist and biologist.

b 'Free writing': Ask the learner to write as much as he can in five minutes. The goal is to keep writing *all the time*. He shouldn't worry about mistakes now.

j 'Free writing' (writing continuously without stopping) for five minutes; just ask the L to keep on writing, whatever the content.

r Show parallels between classroom writing and real-life writing: what the similarities are.

z Teacher calls the learners in to discuss the situation and to ask them to write a new assignment.

c With T guidance, Ls generate their own writing activities, ones which are relevant and interesting to their peers.

k Do pre-writing exercise to brainstorm ways to start paragraphs.

s Practise finding concluding sentences in texts; write own conclusion for existing text by another author.

WILD CARD
Invent a solution for one of the problems posed.

d Vary the readership of the activities: write to real people and organisations (e.g. pen pals, Greenpeace) and get real answers.

l Make writing assignments more personal by writing journal entries, ungraded pieces which learners write for themselves or for other learners to read.

t Read text examples and find details that support generalisation; peers discuss details missing from own writing.

WILD CARD
Invent a solution for one of the problems posed.

e Brainstorm with classmates: discuss everything they know about a topic.

m Vary the genres: write a variety of text types (e.g. personal letter, visa application).

u Ask learners to work in pairs or to write individually, *or*, change the groups so that the learners work with others they want to work with.

WILD CARD
Invent a solution for one of the problems posed.

f Read an article or listen to a tape on the topic. Get additional background information.

n Group writing: work with a group to compose a piece of writing.

v Tell learner to write one paragraph for each idea; have another learner read to check the number of ideas per paragraph in new version.

WILD CARD
Invent a solution for one of the problems posed.

g Let two or three peers read the writing: brainstorm what information is missing that would convince them more.

o Clarify who the audience is and what kind of tone is appropriate: read other texts to identify examples of these; re-write the piece, keeping the audience in mind.

w Practise grammar exercises and punctuation exercises: review rules for composing complete sentences.

WILD CARD
Invent a solution for one of the problems posed.

h Return the piece of writing to the learner and ask for a rewrite. The second draft should focus on the missing information.

p Practise note-taking while reading and/or listening.

x Ask the learner to underline the things seen from the narrator's viewpoint, and circle those seen from another viewpoint. Ask the learner to change the circled ones to be seen from the narrator's viewpoint.

WILD CARD
Invent a solution for one of the problems posed.

Unit 10, Task 2 In unison

Jumbled lesson plan – An integrated skills lesson

a In large, clear letters, Ls write captions for the photos: Ls write about themselves (e.g. *My name's Tomek. I love skating.*) and about the famous people (e.g. *Her name's Madonna. She's American.*) (10 min)

b Discuss completed projects with Ls, give feedback on poster's appearance and use of English language. (5 min)

c Ls make poster: Ls discuss their plan for the design. Remind them to stick to *English*! Groups then stick on photos, captions, add title, decorations. (5-10 min)

d Introduce Ls to project: explain purpose, draw picture of poster on board. (3 min)

e Materials:
- *Mosaic 1* coursebook p16 + T's bk
- photo of each learner brought by Ls
- pictures of famous people brought by Ls
- a few sheets of large paper for posters
- scissors, glue and coloured pens

f Put posters on wall; Ls read other groups' posters. (5 min)

g Ls show other members of their group the captions they have written; group corrects each other's English. (5-10 min)

h Ls get out photos of themselves and their pictures of famous people; Ls break into groups of 5 (10 pictures per poster). (2 min)

i Aims:
- To produce a poster on which every learner has a photo of him/herself with a caption, and a picture of a famous person with captions.
- To revise present tense, possessive adjectives, contractions (*I'm/he's/she's*) and names of countries and nationalities.

Unit 11, Task 2 Taking the plunge and **Task 3 If u kn rd ths**

Henny's story

<u>Woman Found After Two Month</u>

Yesterday old woman was found in her Haus probably she was dead for two month. The neighbours thought she was on a holyday. The woman probably murdered with a book she was hit in the back of her face. The murderer is yet not been found. But the police has a lot of clues.

And some eye witnesses have told the police that the man was shabby and seedy.

Unit 11, Task 4 A bird's eye view and Task 6 Bravo!

Margareta's letter

Dear Jagdeesh,

1 You asked me what I think to be a succesful life. I think it is very difficult to say what a succesful life is. It depended on different kind of people.

2 For somebody a succesful life is a life with wonderful family. Somebody else feels succesful when he has a good and interesting job. It depended on what the people call a succes. If you have a wonderful family and life in comfortable house, somewhere, in the mountains, you feel very happy. But for other people it is too little. They want to get a fascinating job, they want to be admiring, sometimes they want to dominate other people.

3 But for somebody else, f.e. for a poor ~~people,~~ person succes is when he could find or get a slice of bread.

4 A sportsman thinks he reached a succes when he break the record or when he is better than other competitions.

5 I think our life is successful when we live how we want and when we glad it what we do.

6 If we really know what we would like to do in our life we could say that we reached a success.

7 I hope your life is successful. Please write soon.

Yours truly,

Margareta

76

Unit 11, Task 7 Very truly yours

Catalina's journal

Level of L: _____   Age of L: _____

Subject: _____

Example language problem:

_____

Visuals included? Yes/No

If so, whose? _____

What does 'mone' probably mean? _____

Nature of teacher's reply:

content: _____

tone of reply: _____

> *March 24*
>
> *These mone I look at a car hit a cat the litte cat die*
>
> *That is so sad. Did you cry when the car hit the cat? I know I would have cried – the poor little cat.*

Miguel's journal

Level of L: _____   Age of L: _____

Subject: _____

Example language problem:

_____

Visuals included? Yes/No

If so, whose? _____

What does 'pleople' probably mean? _____

What other types of errors does Miguel make?

_____

_____

_____

Nature of teacher's reply:

content: _____

tone of reply: _____

use of L1 (Spanish): _____

length of sentences: _____

> *November*
>
> *Yes meny pleople go to Barcroft (school) Yes mi go in el salvador a big school meny people school in el salvador I like america to yuo like America*
>
> *Yes, I like America very much. What subjects (sujetos) did they teach you in El Salvador? Did you study (Estudiaste) math (matemáticas)? Did you study science (ciencia)? Did you study history (historia)? In Barcroft school you study math. You study science. You study history. You study English.*

Unit 11, Task 8 Tackling it yourself

Tackling it yourself

Sports Island

1 On top of my Island, there are great sports shops.

2 There under, there lives Dennis Bergkamp (a famous footballer).

3 Next of that house, there are another Fila's.

4 Under off my Island, there is a great football stadium.

5 Right of my Island, there are white and big mountains.

6 Next of the mountains, there is a great golf club.

7 Next of the golf club, there is a big basketball club.

8 Come and see this great sports Island. Have a nice Holiday.

Unit 12, Task 4 Whoops!

Observation table: Spoken errors

Class _____ Number of learners _____ Age of learners _____ Length of lesson _____

Level _____ Observer _____ Teacher observed _____

Aims of the lesson _____

_____

_____

Materials used _____

What was the mistake or error made?	Was it corrected? Yes or no	How?	Your remarks
I goed there	Y	T shouted correct form	Unfair: L unaware of irregular verb forms

Unit 12, Task 5 Erroroleplay

Role cards for Erroroleplay (1)

TEACHER 1: MS/MR ALOOF

Your group's task

Give your group exactly ten minutes to complete their task.

Show one member of the group the picture below. S/he must keep it secret and describe it to the others, who draw it. They can ask questions for clarification, but cannot see the picture. Stop the activity after 10 minutes, when the picture can then be revealed to the group.

Your role

You are a teacher who does not intervene at all in the activity. After setting up your activity, and making sure all participants understand, sit at a table apart from the group and pretend you have nothing to do with the group. Ignore them and do not correct any errors.

Unit 12, Task 5 Erroroleplay

Role cards for Erroroleplay (2)

TEACHER 2: MS/MR ZEAL

Your group's task

Give your group exactly ten minutes to complete their task.

Explain to them that in half an hour the earth is going to be totally destroyed. All the members of your group have secured places in a rocket which is to take off in 10 minutes' time and which contains enough food and fuel for 30 years. There are four people outside the rocket who want to take up the final place in the rocket. Your group must decide which of the following people to take: it must be a unanimous decision and you can only choose one extra person. Show your group the information below.

The four people are:

1 Meena: woman aged 27, pregnant, Pakistani; doctorate in Food Science, good cook, in good health.

2 Harry: man aged 23, nurse, American, qualified in general medical and psychiatric nursing.

3 Ola: teenage girl aged 16, Australian, very knowledgeable about science, enthusiastic about life.

4 Tim: science student aged 24, Nigerian, knowledgeable about computers and spacecraft; gregarious.

Your role

You enjoy the activity so much that you join in. You forget about errors and don't correct anyone.

TEACHER 3: MS/MR BUSYBODY

Your group's task

Give your group exactly ten minutes to complete their task.

Each of group members looks at a different set of pictures, numbered 1-4, which they must not show each other. If you have more than 4 people in your group, some people can talk about the same set of pictures. Their task is to discover which of them have the same picture(s). (Only two of the total number of pictures are the same, but don't tell them that!) Stop the group after 10 minutes if they haven't finished.

Key

The two identical pictures are pictures *f* and *n*.

Your role

Intervene as much as you can, correcting people's errors as they make them. Be as aggressive and bossy as you can; interrupt as many times as possible, correcting language errors.

Unit 12, Task 5 Erroroleplay

Role cards for Erroroleplay (3)

TEACHER 4: MS/MR EAVESDROP

Your group's task

Give your group exactly ten minutes to complete their task.

Your group should write a list of ten pieces of advice for a new teacher about correcting spoken errors.

Your role

Make a note of the language errors the learners make as they occur. Just before the end of their task, stop them and take a few minutes to tell the group about their errors.

LEARNER ROLE: MS/MR CATNAP

You had a really bad night and don't feel much like English today. Make lots of language errors as you do every activity. Make sure you do this for *every* activity and for *every* teacher who teaches you.

Unit 12, Task 5 Erroroleplay

Role cards for Erroroleplay (4)

Unit 13, Task 3 Deduce the lesson plan

Observation table: Deduce the lesson plan

Class _____   Number of learners _____   Age of learners _____   Length of lesson _____

Level _____   Observer _____   Teacher observed _____

Aims of the lesson _____

_____

_____

Materials used _____

Aim	What teacher does	What learners do	Materials	Grouping	Timing
Introduction to a reading topic	Gives out photos	Describe photos to each other; discuss newspaper article that might accompany it	8 copies of photo: 1 per group	fours	10 min

Unit 13, Task 4 Topsy-turvy

Jumbled lesson plan

---

a Listen to tape (TS48); Ls listen and check answers.

---

b Revision. *Do you have Maths on Thursdays? English on Fridays?* (etc.)   T→Ls

---

c Materials: *Fountain Beginners* Unit 8 no. 9 p.50
               Tape recorder and cassette (TS48)

---

d Tell Ls about what I do on Sundays.   T→Ls
Ask some Ls *What do you do on Sundays?*

---

e Ask Ls about each cartoon picture (avoid present continuous);   T→Ls
use vocab from other units. E.g. pic 1 *Where's Dan?*
Is Joe in bed? etc.

---

f Intro task. Match Joe and Dan to sentences a–p in bk.   PAIRS
Do example with class picture 1: Dan (i) and Joe (h)

---

g Aims: Ls revise vocabulary of names of school subjects
           Ls practise intensive listening
           Ls revise present simple tense for everyday activities

---

h p.50 CB. Intro Dan and Joe King: Joe = artist (glasses);   T→Ls
Dan = student. Typical Sunday: cartoon shows what Joe
and Dan do on Sundays (every Sunday)

Unit 13, Task 7 Lesson planning snakes and ladders

Game cards (1)

TEACHER CARD You feel a bit ill today.	**TEACHER CARD** A colleague taught the previous lesson and should have taught your class how to use the present continuous tense. Halfway through your lesson, you realise that he did not do that.	**SURPRISE CARD** It's extremely hot today and your learners say they don't feel like doing English.
TEACHER CARD You left your lesson plan at home on your desk.	**TEACHER CARD** You have forgotten to bring your chalk and you need to use the blackboard for a presentation.	**SURPRISE CARD** It's the last day before a major holiday and no-one wants to do the last exercises in the book.
TEACHER CARD You have five minutes before the lesson ends and you have nothing left to do.	**TEACHER CARD** You are teaching a listening lesson. You thought you had found the place on the tape beforehand, but you get hopelessly lost and can't find the text.	**SURPRISE CARD** You are about to teach a lesson on reading but have just heard that the director will visit your class in order to hear how well the students can converse.
TEACHER CARD A colleague has to meet a parent and asks you to take over her 40-minute lesson just five minutes before it starts.	**TEACHER CARD** You heard just before the lesson that one of the learners in the class has had an accident and is in hospital.	**SURPRISE CARD** About ten minutes into the lesson, three learners arrive late. They say they have been in the head teacher's office.
TEACHER CARD You have over-planned and you haven't managed to cover everything in your lesson plan.	**TEACHER CARD** You suddenly realise you forgot to copy an important text for the class.	**SURPRISE CARD** The photocopier has broken down and you couldn't copy vital material for your lesson.

See also Game cards (2) on page 88.

86

Unit 13, Task 7 Lesson planning
snakes and ladders

Rules

1 Play in groups of 4-6.

2 Everyone puts their counters together on the square, THE START OF THE LESSON.

3 Throw the dice: the highest scorer begins.

4 The first player throws the dice. If you throw 4, move your counter 4 squares, if you throw 3, move 3 squares, etc.

5 If you land on a Teacher square, take a TEACHER CARD; if you land on a Learner square, take a LEARNER CARD, and so on. Give a possible solution to the problem that you find on your card. If everyone in your group accepts your solution, you can stay where you are; if it is not a satisfactory solution, you must return to where you were on your previous turn.

6 If you land at the bottom of a ladder, you climb to the top. If you land on the head of a snake, you must slide down to the bottom of the snake.

7 The winner is the player who reaches THE END OF THE LESSON first.

36 Surprise

35 Teacher

26 Learner

37 Learner

34 Learner

27 Your lesson is so well-planned it goes brilliantly

38 Teacher

33 Learner

28 Surprise

39 The fire bell rings

32 Surprise

29 Learner

The end of the lesson

40 Teacher

31 Teacher

30 Everyone is sent home early because of dreadful weather

The start of the lesson

1 Teacher
2 It's your birthday and your class is behaving perfectly
3 Learner
4 Surprise
5 Teacher
6 Teacher
7 Learner
8 Surprise
9 Teacher
10 Your learners ask for an extra lesson
11 Surprise
12 Learner
13 Teacher
14 Learner
15 Teacher
16 An important visitor arrives and all the lessons are cancelled
17 Surprise
18 Learner
19 Teacher
20 Teacher
21 Surprise
22 Learner
23 Surprise
24 Teacher
25 Surprise

Unit 13, Task 7 Lesson planning snakes and ladders

Game cards (2)

SURPRISE CARD The video recorder works with picture only, no sound.	**LEARNER CARD** Your class is doing a pair work activity using past tense questions; you suddenly realise that they are making lots of mistakes.	**LEARNER CARD** You draw a picture on the blackboard but the learners don't understand it.
SURPRISE CARD You are called to the telephone in the middle of your lesson.	**LEARNER CARD** One of your learners says she feels ill and wants to leave the room.	**LEARNER CARD** Over half of your learners have not brought their books to the lesson.
SURPRISE CARD It's snowing really heavily today and public transport has come to a standstill; half of the learners are late or not coming today.	**LEARNER CARD** As you are setting up a group work activity, to last for half of your lesson, the class tells you they have done it before.	**LEARNER CARD** You based a part of your lesson on homework, but over half the class hasn't done the homework you set.
SURPRISE CARD Your learners had some tough exams yesterday and don't feel like English today.	**LEARNER CARD** Just before your lesson, you hear that half of the class is absent; they are re-taking a test in another subject.	**LEARNER CARD** Halfway through your lesson, a learner points out that you forgot to correct the homework which they prepared for today.
SURPRISE CARD Someone was supposed to copy a text for you but she forgot; you have to teach the lesson without that text.	**LEARNER CARD** One of your learners doesn't understand your explanation about the future tense; you feel you are wasting precious lesson time.	**LEARNER CARD** Three learners have forgotten to bring a pen or pencil to your lesson.

Unit 14, Task 3 Silent movie

Silent movie cards

past tense (thumb/hand/arm)	**indicate 'here'** (finger/hand)	**'write it on the board'** (any body part and chalk)	**'that's wrong'** (face)
future tense (index finger/ hand/arm)	**'stop'** (hands)	**'don't show your picture to anyone'** (any body part)	**'you must divide in half'** (arms/hands)
'nearly' (hand/face)	**indicate 'there'** (finger/hand)	**'come here'** (arm/hand)	**'that's wrong'** (head)
'repeat in chorus' (arms)	**connect two words** (fingers/hands)	**'it's your turn'** (arm/hand)	**'good'** (fingers/hand)
'repeat individually' (hand/arm)	**'good'** (face)	**'that's incorrect'** (finger/hand)	**'repeat individually'** (head/eyes)
'get into pairs' (arm/hand/fingers)	**'you must divide into groups of 3'** (hands/arms/fingers)	**'not quite right'** (face)	**'you must divide into groups of 4'** (hands/arms/fingers)

Unit 15, Task 1 Curtain up

Questionnaire: Learning styles[1]

1 Write the score that most applies to you next to each sentence below:

| 5 – almost always |
| 4 – fairly often |
| 3 – sometimes |
| 2 – rarely |
| 1 – almost never |

Score   Statement

_____ 1 It helps me understand if I discuss things with other people.

_____ 2 When learning, I watch the teacher's face a lot.

_____ 3 I use colours when I take down notes or read (e.g. highlighter pens, different coloured pens).

_____ 4 I get good ideas while I am doing some kind of physical activity.

_____ 5 I prefer spoken to written instructions.

_____ 6 I'd rather listen to a tape than read about a topic.

_____ 7 I prefer someone to draw me a map than to tell me directions to somewhere.

_____ 8 I do less well on written tests than on oral tests.

_____ 9 I don't like sitting at a desk, but study, for example, on the floor, on the bed, in all kinds of places.

_____ 10 I take notes but they are a bit of a mess.

_____ 11 I can easily understand maps, charts, graphs, etc.

_____ 12 I can't sit still for very long.

_____ 13 I like making things with my hands.

_____ 14 If I am doing some work, having the radio on annoys me.

_____ 15 I like to take a lot of breaks when I study.

_____ 16 I use a lot of body language (e.g. gestures) when talking.

_____ 17 I can't picture things in my head very well.

_____ 18 I would rather start doing an activity instead of listening to instructions about how to do it.

_____ 19 I like telling jokes and can remember them well.

_____ 20 I take lots of notes when I read or listen to a lecture.

_____ 21 I doodle when I listen to a lecture.

_____ 22 If I don't look at a speaker, I can still follow well what he or she is saying.

_____ 23 I like creating models of what I am learning.

_____ 24 In a test, I can visualise the place on the page where I learnt something.

_____ 25 I like making projects better than writing reports.

_____ 26 I like to talk when I write.

_____ 27 If I read, I 'listen' to the words in my head.

_____ 28 If I write something down, I remember it better.

_____ 29 I can't remember what people look like very well; I remember better what they say.

_____ 30 If I want to remember something, for example someone's telephone number, it helps if I make a picture of it in my head.

_____ 31 If I study aloud, I can remember better.

_____ 32 I can see pictures in my head.

_____ 33 I would rather read than be read to.

2 Transfer your scores and add them up:

2 _____	4 _____	1 _____
3 _____	9 _____	5 _____
7 _____	10 _____	6 _____
11 _____	12 _____	8 _____
14 _____	13 _____	17 _____
20 _____	15 _____	19 _____
24 _____	16 _____	22 _____
28 _____	18 _____	26 _____
30 _____	21 _____	27 _____
32 _____	23 _____	29 _____
33 _____	25 _____	31 _____
Visual learner	**Kinaesthetic learner**	**Auditory learner**
Total score:	**Total score:**	**Total score:**
_____	_____	_____

Your highest score indicates which your strongest learning style is, your lowest score shows your weakest. There is no right, or perfect, learning style: everyone is, to some degree, a mixture of all three learning styles, but most people may have one learning style which is dominant. A score of more than 40 indicates a particularly strong style; a score of under 20 indicates quite a weak style.

[1] This Learning Styles questionnaire was inspired by those in Reid, 1995.

Unit 15, Task 7 Virtual reality

Virtual reality role cards

Simulation 1: Role A   An English learner

You are a 16-year-old and you have been called in to see your new teacher and you don't know why. You suspect it has something to do with your behaviour in class, but you have a genuinely good excuse for your behaviour.

Wait for your teacher to begin the conversation.

Simulation 1: Role B   An observer

You are observing a conversation between an EFL teacher and a learner, who has been called in to explain his/her classroom behaviour. As you observe, make notes on the following:

- the tone of the conversation (friendly, accusatory, etc.)
- the ability of each party to listen and accept an opinion that is different from their own
- the way each person tries to persuade the other
- the most interesting thing you observed

Afterwards, briefly discuss what you noted down with the other members of your group.

Simulation 2: Role A   An observer

You are observing a conversation between a director of a teacher training course and a native speaker teacher of reading skills on the course, regarding several complaints from students about his/her teaching. As you observe, make notes on the following:

- the tone of the conversation (friendly, accusatory, etc.)
- the ability of each party to listen and accept an opinion that is different from their own
- the way each person tries to persuade the other
- the most interesting thing you observed

Afterwards, briefly discuss what you noted down with the other members of your group.

Simulation 2: Role B
A teacher training director

Earlier this year, you hired an enthusiastic native speaker EFL teacher to teach reading skills. Halfway through this term, three student representatives from three of this teacher's reading classes complained to you on three separate occasions about his/her bad teaching. You have also heard, from reliable sources, that this teacher has gone out to local discos and clubs with students. You have called this teacher in to your office to discuss the situation with him/her.

Start the conversation.

Simulation 3: Role A   A teacher trainer

You are having a compulsory meeting with a teacher trainee whom you have observed and you do not like personally. The trainee has come to discuss a recent experience of working with a class of 30 intermediate-level 14-year-olds in a public secondary school. In courses with your trainees you have been enthusiastic about teaching communicatively and you continue to promote this now as a supervisor on teaching practice.

Begin the conversation.

Simulation 3: Role B   A teacher trainee

You recently tried to use a communicative activity with your class of 30 intermediate-level 14-year-olds and it was a complete failure. Previously, you had been enthusiastic about communicative teaching, but now you lack confidence about teaching that way. You are having a compulsory meeting with your supervisor, who always intimidates you. Discuss the general situation and your specific problems.

(Before the simulation begins, think of a specific communicative activity to discuss.)

Wait for your supervisor to begin the conversation.

Unit 15, Task 7 Virtual reality

Virtual reality role cards

Simulation 1: Role C   An EFL teacher

You are a new student teacher. You have called in one of your 16-year-old EFL learners to discuss with him/her some problematic classroom behaviour. Investigate the source of the problem and resolve it.

(Before the simulation begins, think of a specific behaviour problem to deal with.)

Begin the conversation.

Simulation 2: Role C
A native speaker EFL teacher

You are a native speaker EFL teacher, teaching reading skills on a teacher training course abroad. You arrived in this country less than two months ago and now teach several reading classes with different groups. From time to time you go to local clubs and discos with your students and you think you are pretty popular. The course director has asked you to come and speak to him/her privately.

Wait for the director to start the conversation.

Simulation 3: Role C   An observer

You are observing a conversation between a supervisor of teaching practice and a teacher trainee that takes place recently after a bad classroom experience with the trainee's 30 intermediate-level 14-year-old English learners. As you observe, make notes on the following:

- the tone of the conversation (friendly, accusatory, etc.)
- the ability of each party to listen and accept an opinion that is different from their own
- the way each person tries to persuade the other
- the most interesting thing you observed

Afterwards, briefly discuss what you noted down with the other members of your group.

Unit 15, Task 8 Actions and reactions

Actions and reactions role cards

1 Look dreamily out of the window during the lesson.

7 Cooperate with your teacher during the lesson.

2 Put your hand up to answer as many questions as possible.

8 Behave perfectly during the lesson.

3 Talk to your neighbour continually. If you are moved away from your neighbour, keep quiet.

9 Do some other work during this lesson and don't listen.

4 For three minutes of the lesson, answer out of turn.

10 For the instruction stage of the lesson, ask a lot of questions: you don't know what you must do.

5 Behave perfectly during the lesson.

11 Cooperate with your teacher during the lesson.

6 Say nothing unless the teacher addresses you by name.

12 Stand up and move around once during the lesson.

Unit 16, Task 1 Straight from the horse's mouth

Interview: Coursebook analysis

	Teacher 1	Teacher 2
1 Name one coursebook you use now to teach English (author/title).		
2 What class it is used for (Ls' age/English level)?		
3 Which two aspects of the book do you like the most?	*a* *b*	*a* *b*
4 Which two aspects of the book do you dislike most?	*a* *b*	*a* *b*
5 What do the Ls like about this book?		
6 What do the Ls dislike about this book?		
7 How and why was this book chosen for your Ls?		
8 In your opinion, what are the three most important things in selecting a coursebook?	*a* *b* *c*	*a* *b* *c*
9 What other supplementary materials are available (e.g. workbook)? How useful do you find these?		
10 Any other comments?		

Unit 16, Task 2 At first glance

Coursebook evaluation chart

Title:

Author:

Publisher:

Publication Date:

Your initial gut reaction:

The MATERIALS Test	Your comments:	Score 4 = ideal 3 = acceptable 2 = poor 1 = unacceptable
M Method		
A Appearance		
T Teacher-friendly		
E Extras		
R Realistic		
I Interesting		
A Affordable		
L Level		
S Skills		
Total score:		
Assessment according to the key:		

Assessment Key

28–36 = ideal
19–27 = acceptable
10–18 = poor
 1–9 = unacceptable

Unit 16, Task 4 Upon closer inspection

Table: Inspecting activities

	Mosaic I Activities
I Skills work	
a listening	
b speaking	*Activities 1b,*
c reading	
d writing	*Activities 4,*
e grammar	
f pronunciation	
g vocabulary	
II Real communicative interaction	
III Learner interest: likely to motivate Ls	
IV Aims of the unit (from the teacher's manual)	—*present and practise to be with she/he* —*present and practise countries and nationalities*